Seeing Like a Computer

Facebook's Automatic Alternative Text

unknown
UNKNOWNS

Published by
Unknown Unknowns
New York, NY

August 2018

unknownunknowns.org

ISBN-13: 978-0-9913923-3-9

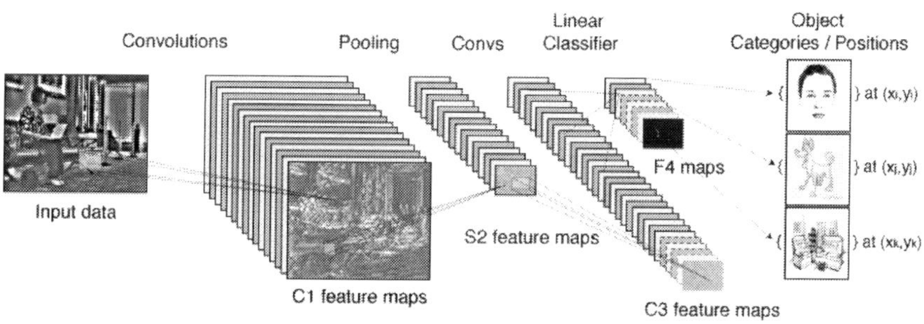

DIAGRAM OF CONVOLUTIONAL NEURAL NETWORK USED FOR IMAGE CLASSIFICATION

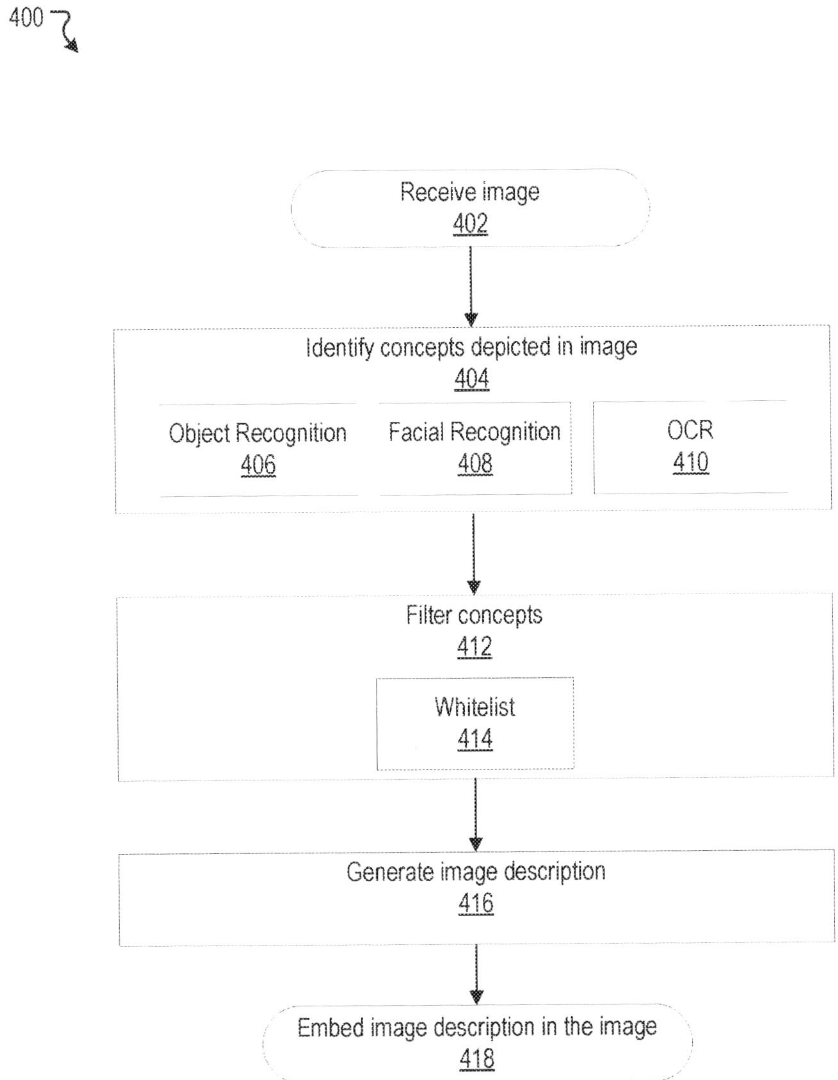

FIGURE 4

DIAGRAM FROM FACEBOOK INC. PATENT
US20180181832A1
SYSTEMS AND METHODS FOR IMAGE
DESCRIPTION GENERATION

In 2016, Facebook's Accessibility team released an automated solution for image captions called Automatic Alternative Text. The goal of the feature was to provide more context to visually impaired users who rely on screen readers to interact with Facebook. While these computationally generated texts are not visible on the interface, they can be found in the image alt tag of the page's HTML code.*

Automatic image recognition and captioning by computers are still limited. The tasks involve many nuances that are difficult for a computer to emulate. While it is easy to mock the inaccurate results of these complex computational tasks, it is more poignant to consider the descriptors that never show up and presumably do not exist in the original training data. In a preliminary test, a riot with heavy police presence is described as "one or more people, people standing, and outdoor." As one might expect from a website where interactions revolve around a "like" button, smiling people are recognized while an image of a person grieving is described as "1 person, sitting, ring and closeup."

The following pages document images and their Automatic Alternative Text from Mark Zuckerberg's Facebook Wall from 2016-2018. The suggested captions compliment the optimistic and welcoming persona of Facebook's founder while literally and figuratively hiding from view important content and context.

*See appendix at back of book for screen captures and example data.

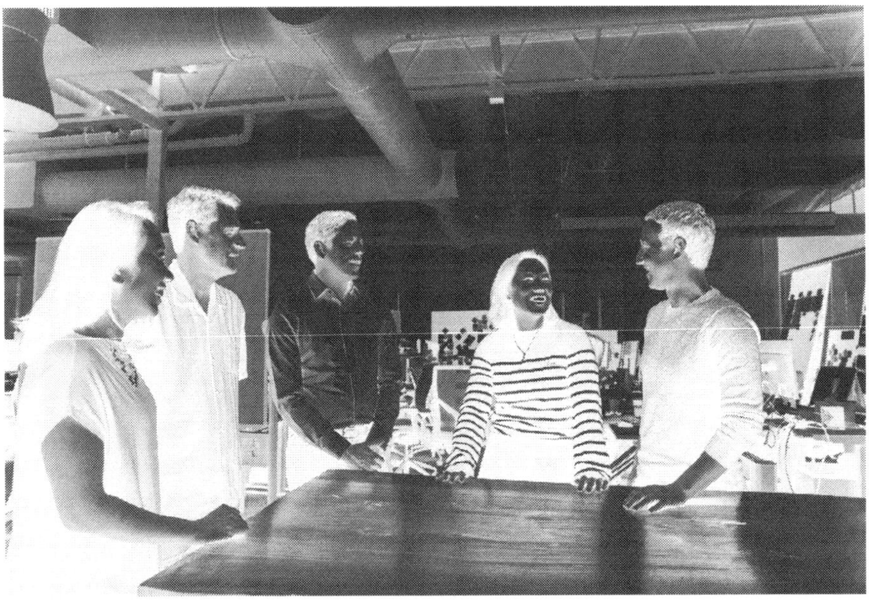

5 PEOPLE, PEOPLE SMILING, PEOPLE SITTING AND INDOOR

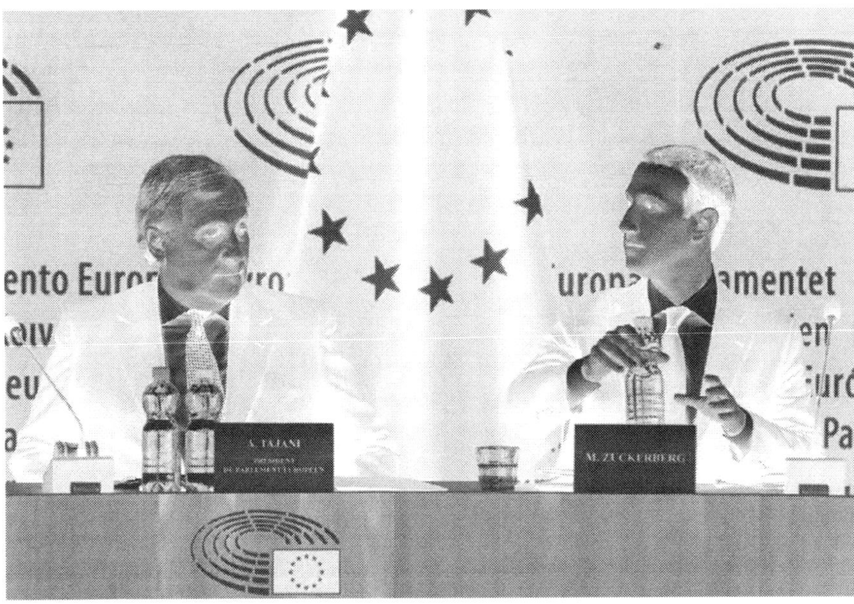
A. TAJANI
M. ZUCKERBERG

2 PEOPLE, PEOPLE STANDING

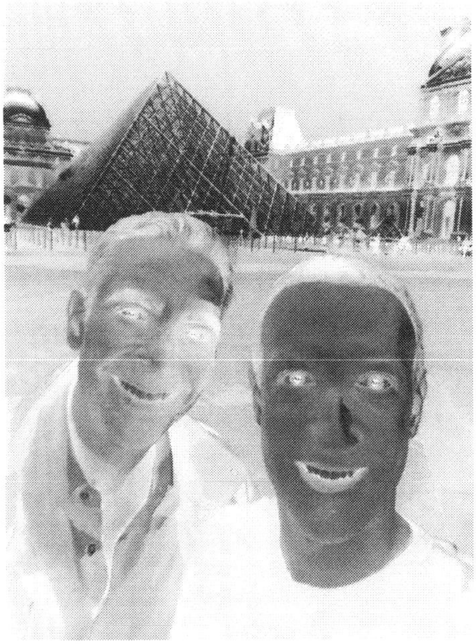

2 PEOPLE, PEOPLE SMILING, CLOSEUP

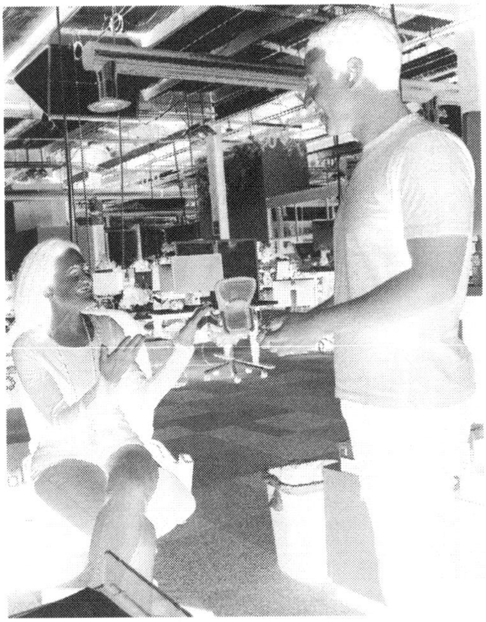

2 PEOPLE, PEOPLE SMILING, PEOPLE SITTING AND INDOOR

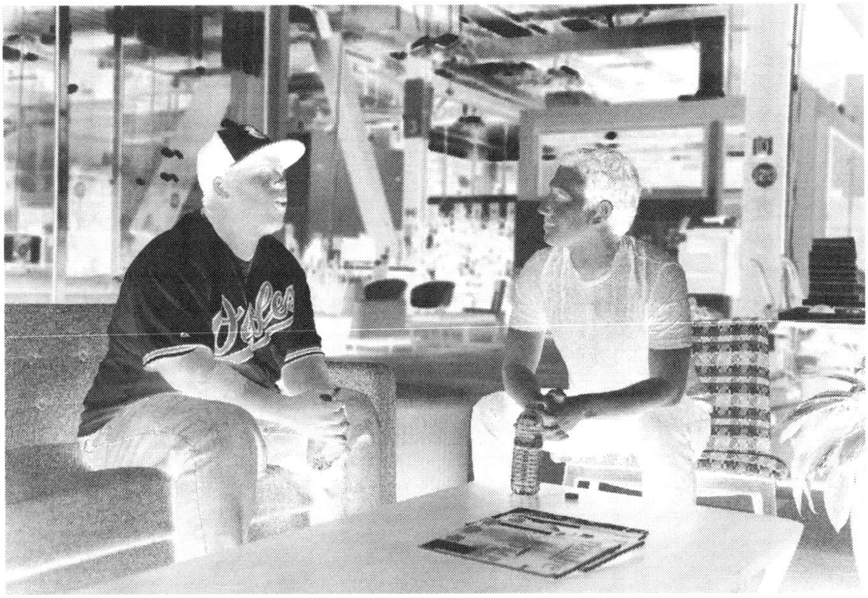

2 PEOPLE, PEOPLE SITTING, TABLE AND OUTDOOR

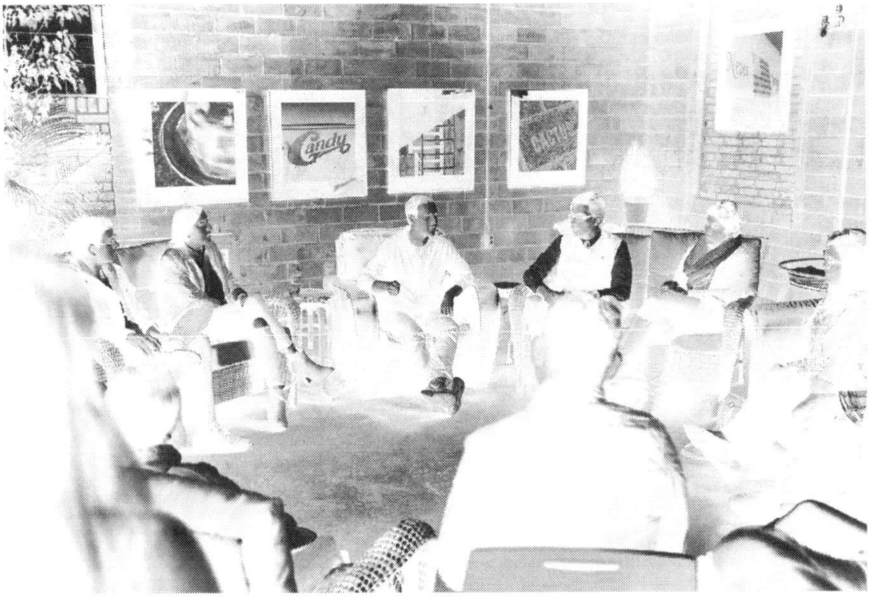
Candy

5 PEOPLE, PEOPLE SITTING AND INDOOR

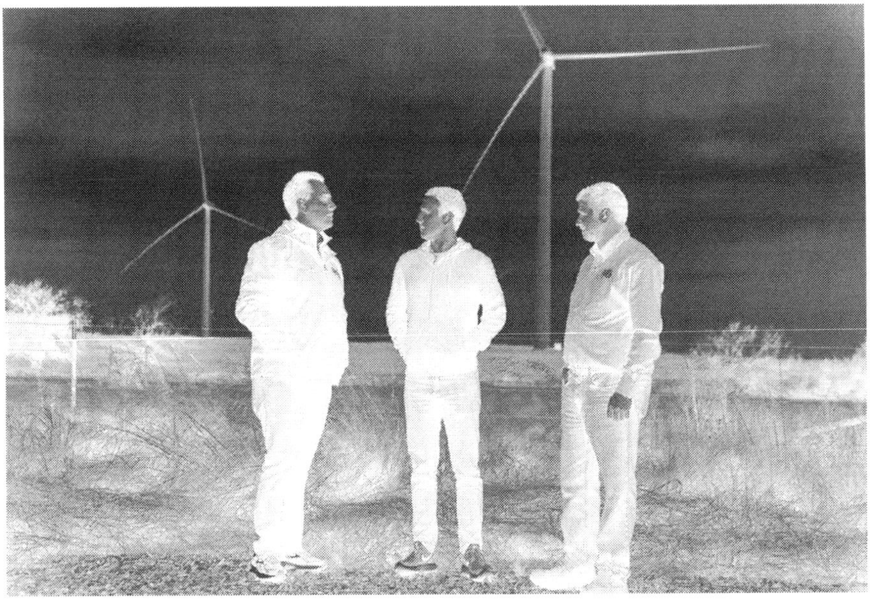

3 PEOPLE, PEOPLE STANDING, SKY, CLOUD,
SHOES, OUTDOOR AND NATURE

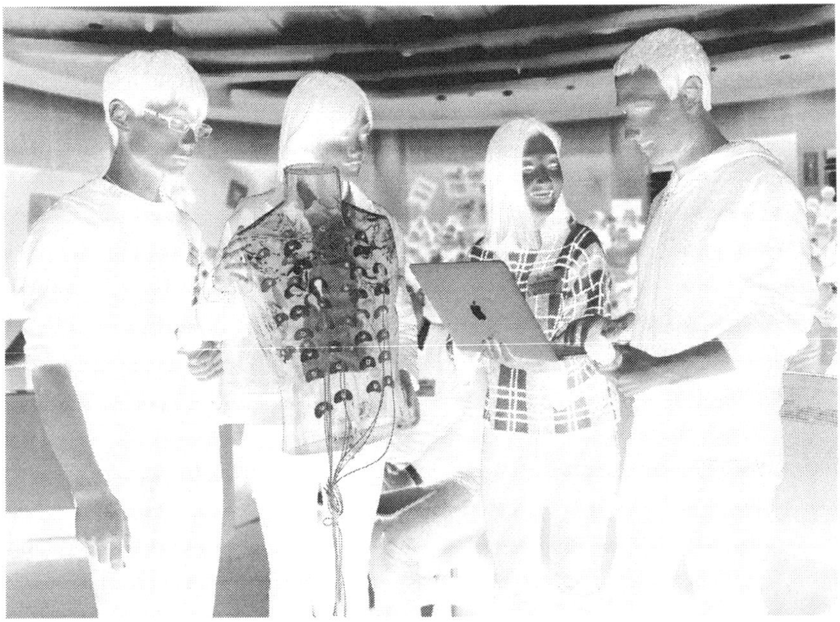

3 PEOPLE, PEOPLE SMILING, PEOPLE STANDING

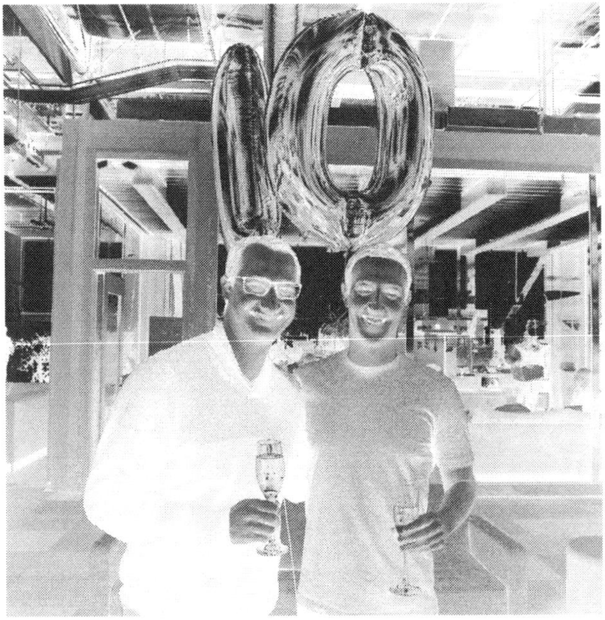

2 PEOPLE, PEOPLE SMILING

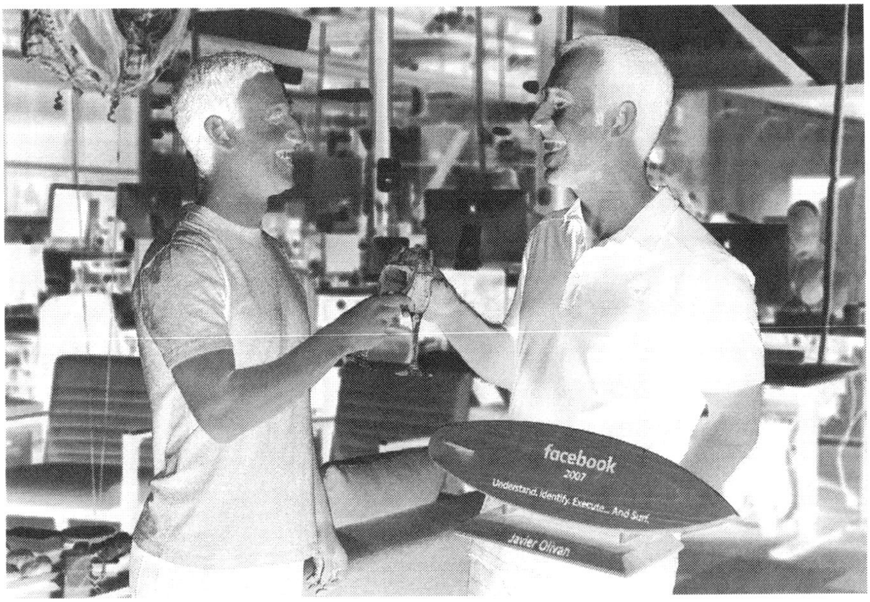
facebook
2007
Understand. Identify. Execute... And Surf.
Javier Olivan

2 PEOPLE

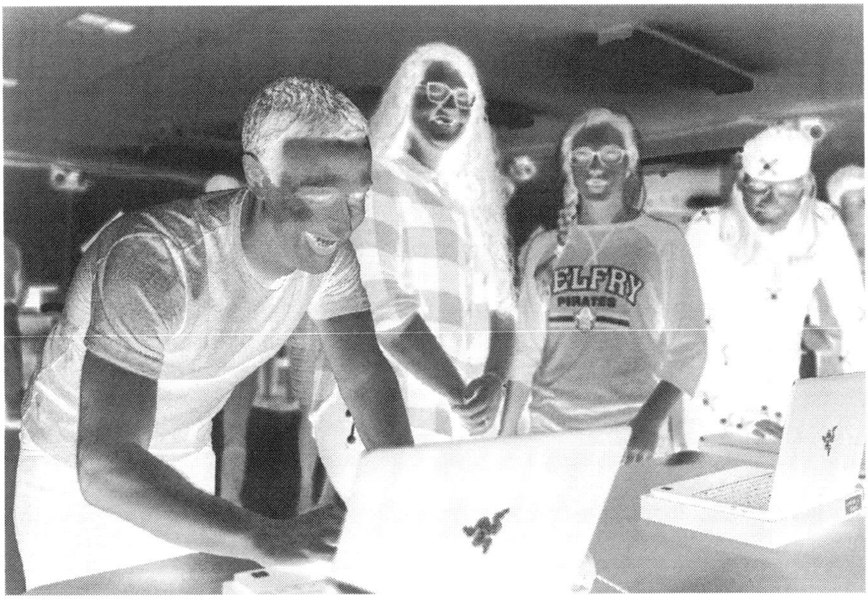
ELFRY
PIRATES

3 PEOPLE, PEOPLE SMILING, PEOPLE SITTING, LAPTOP AND INDOOR

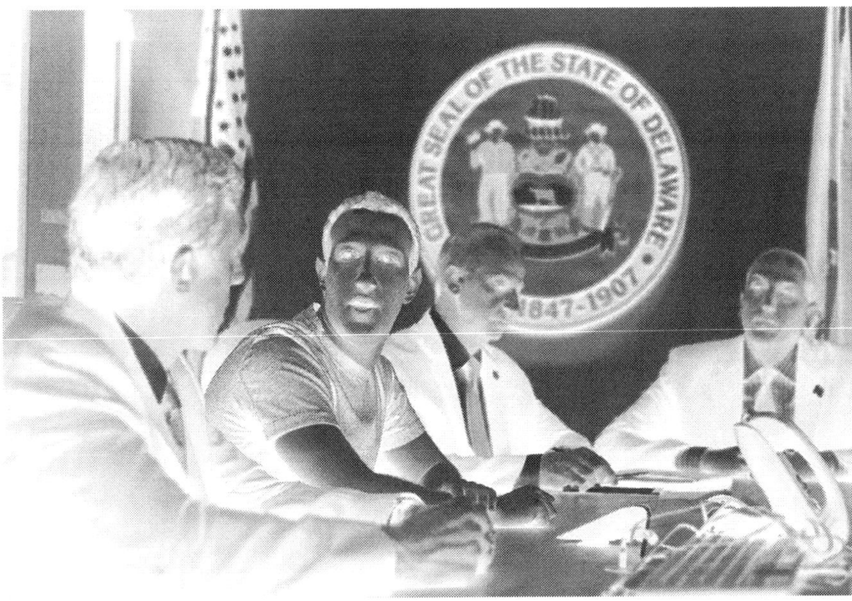
GREAT SEAL OF THE STATE OF DELAWARE
1847-1907

3 PEOPLE, PEOPLE SITTING AND INDOOR

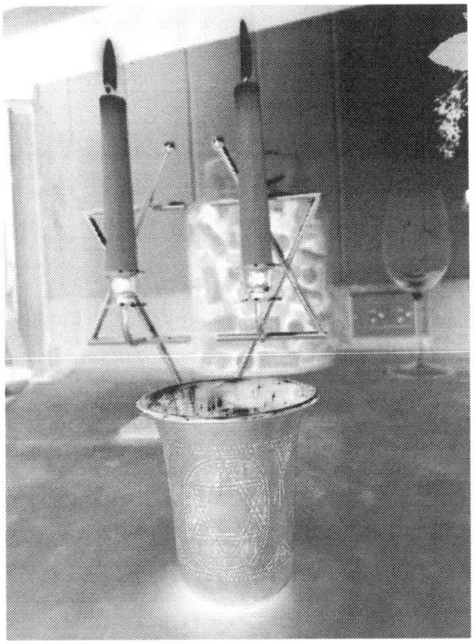

INDOOR

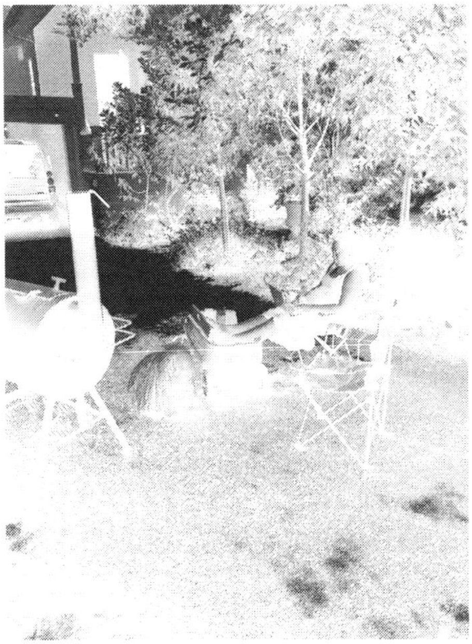

1 PERSON, SITTING, TREE, TABLE, PLANT AND OUTDOOR

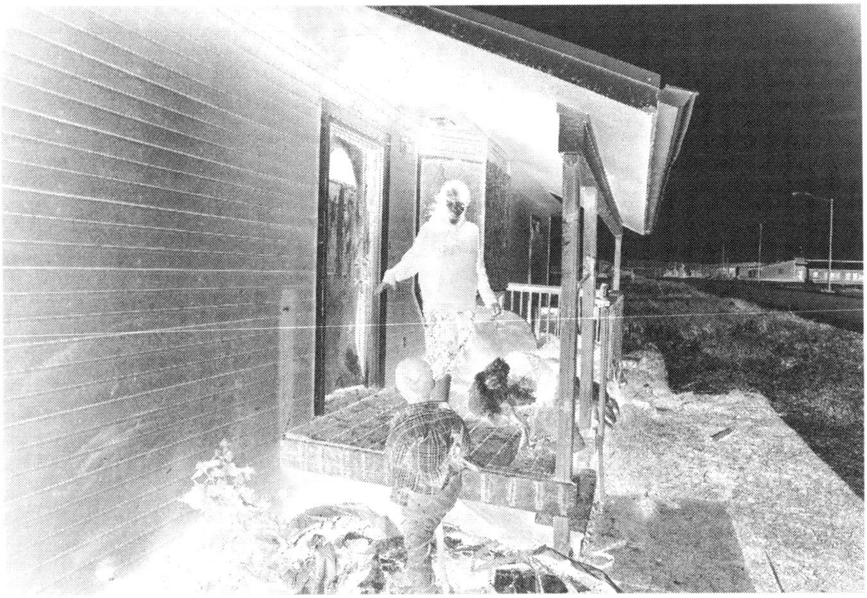

ONE OR MORE PEOPLE AND OUTDOOR

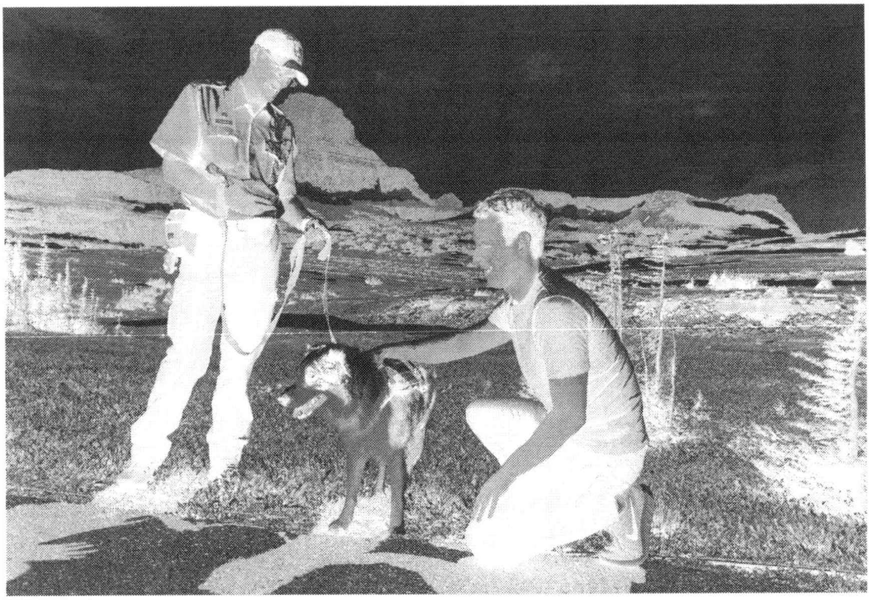

1 PERSON, DOG, SKY, MOUNTAIN, OUTDOOR AND NATURE

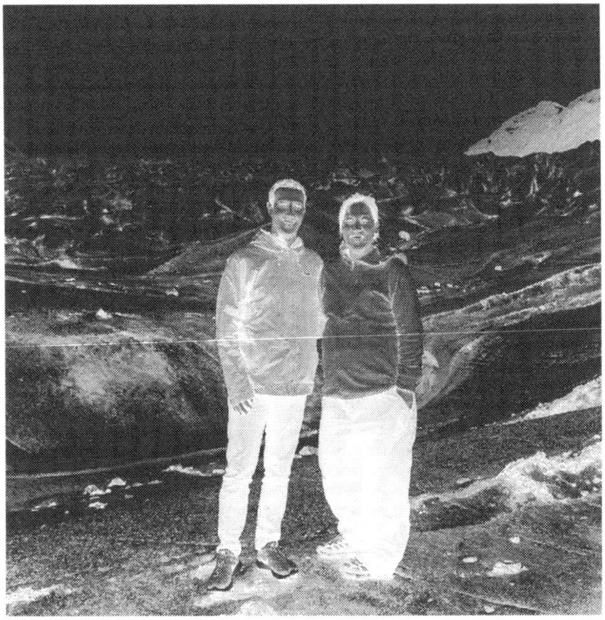

2 PEOPLE, PEOPLE SMILING, PEOPLE
STANDING, SKY, SNOW, MOUNTAIN, OUTDOOR
AND NATURE

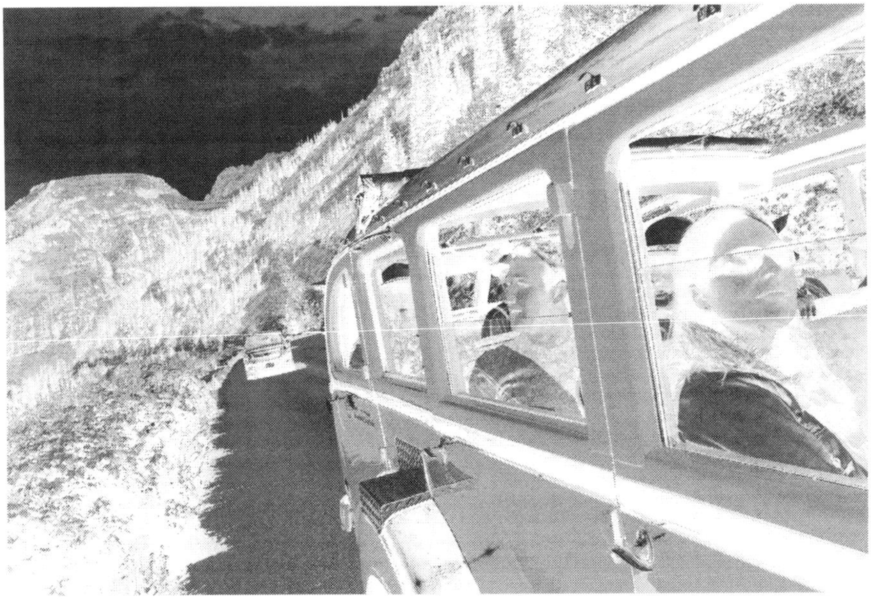

2 PEOPLE, MOUNTAIN, SKY, OUTDOOR AND NATURE

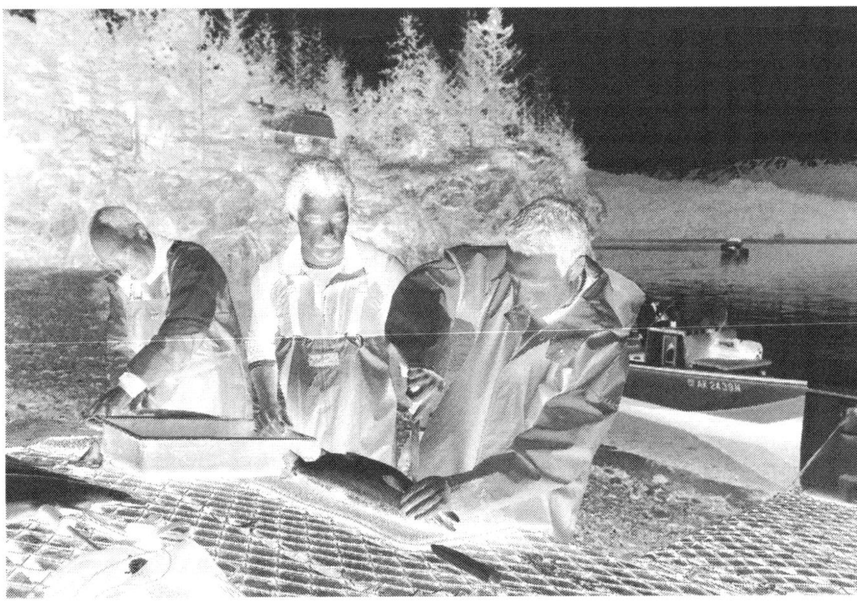

1 PERSON, SITTING, CHILD, TABLE, OUTDOOR, WATER AND FOOD

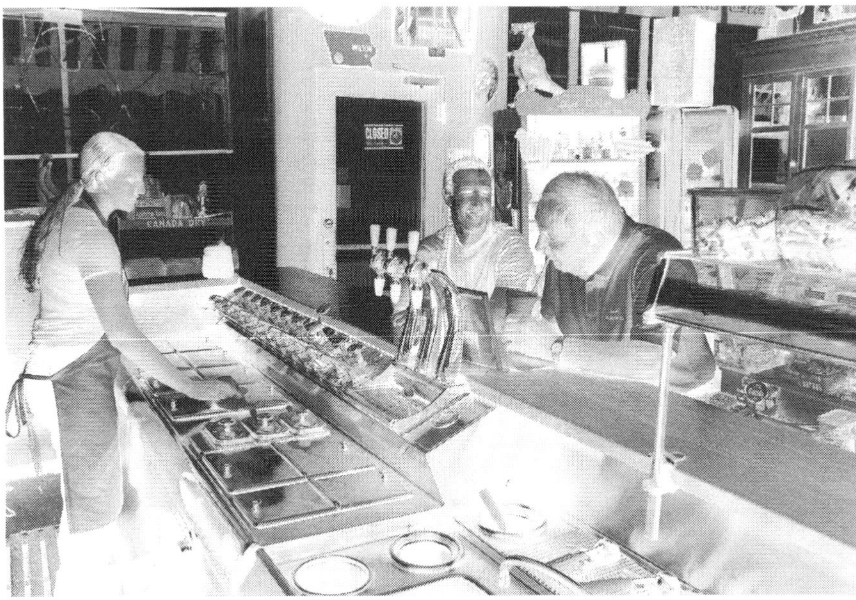
CLOSED
CANADA DRY

2 PEOPLE, PEOPLE SMILING, PEOPLE SITTING, TABLE, INDOOR AND FOOD

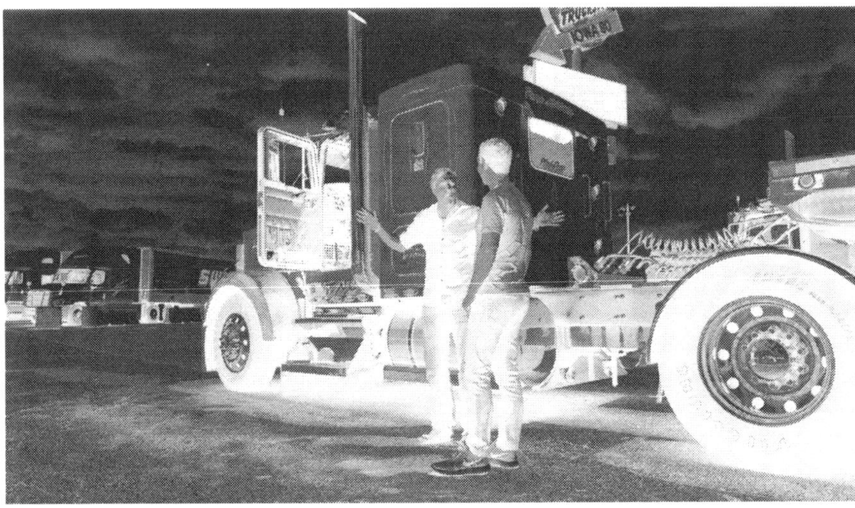

1 PERSON, SKY AND OUTDOOR

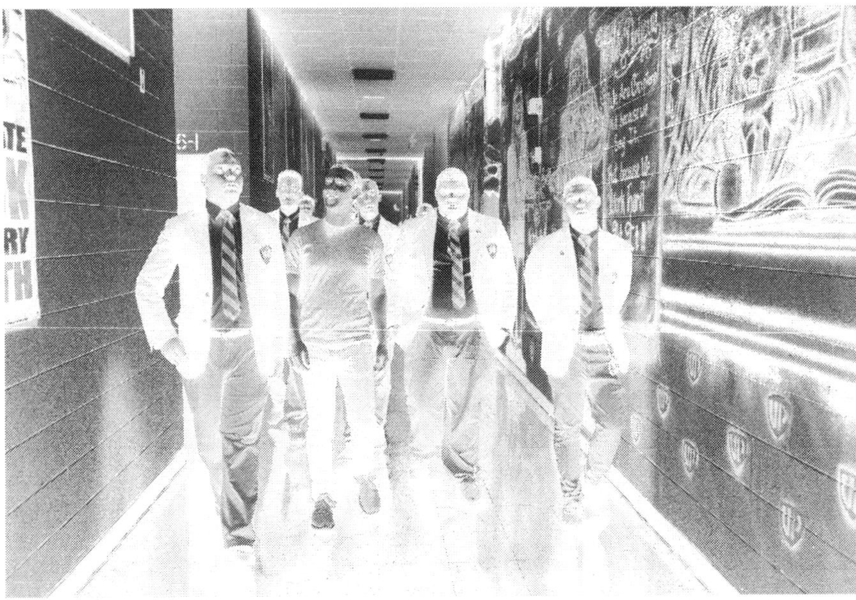

6 PEOPLE, PEOPLE SMILING, PEOPLE STANDING AND INDOOR

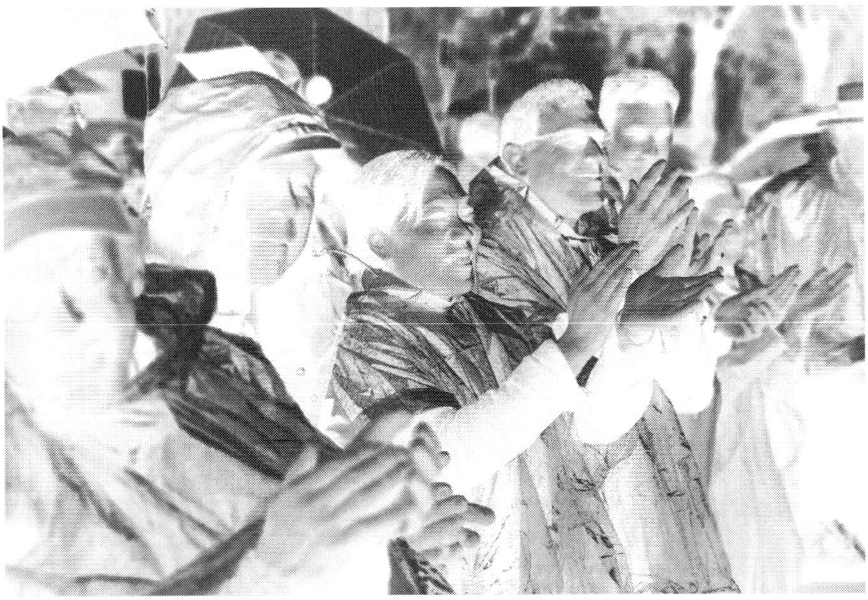

5 PEOPLE, PEOPLE SMILING, OUTDOOR

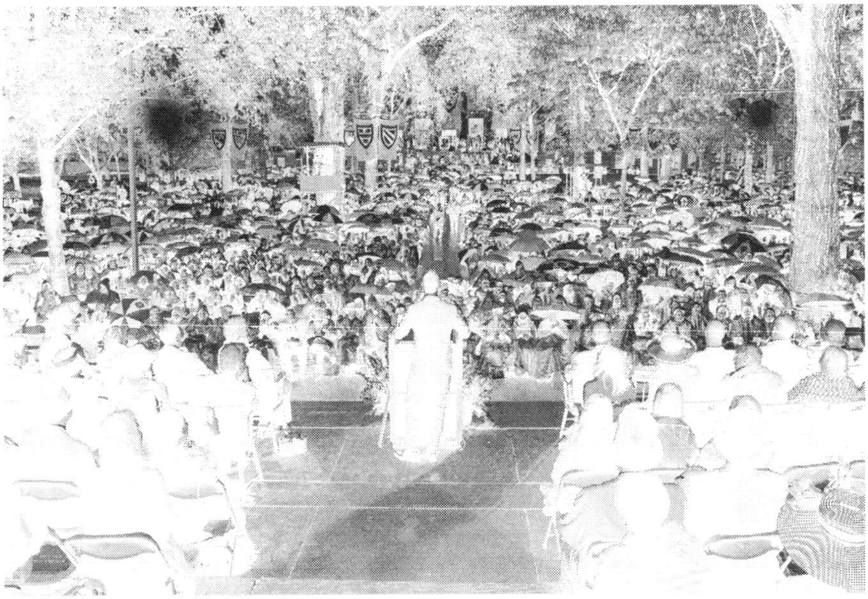

ONE OR MORE PEOPLE, CROWD, TREE AND OUTDOOR

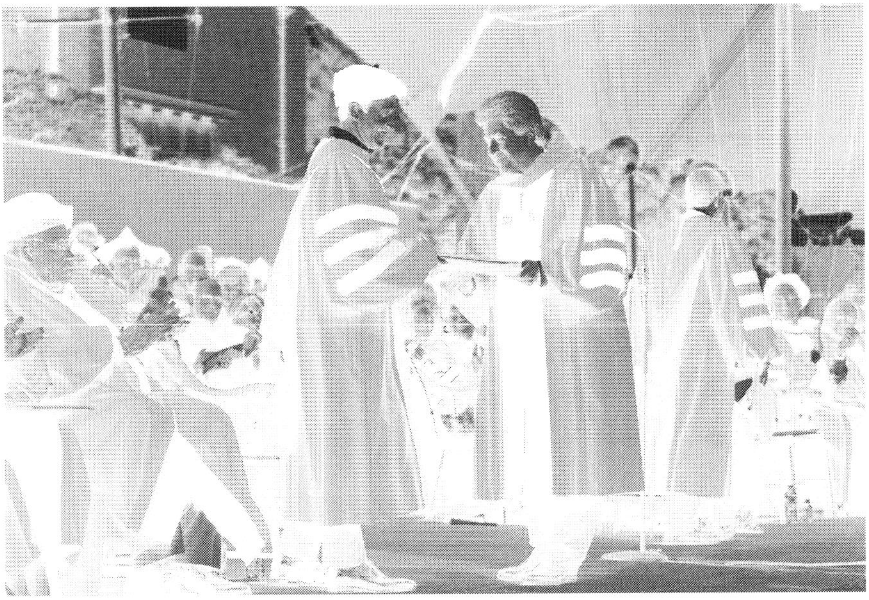

6 PEOPLE, PEOPLE SMILING, PEOPLE STANDING

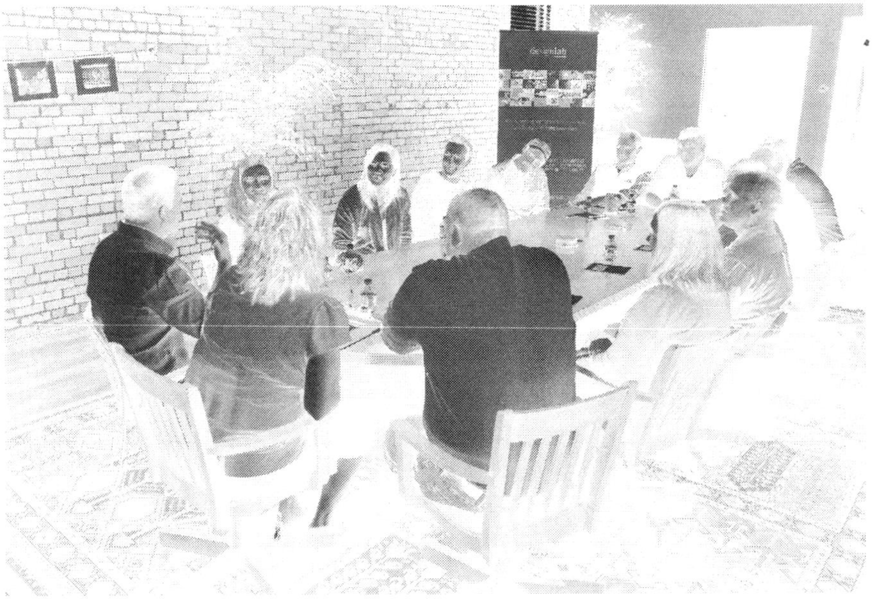

7 PEOPLE, PEOPLE SMILING, PEOPLE SITTING, TABLE AND INDOOR

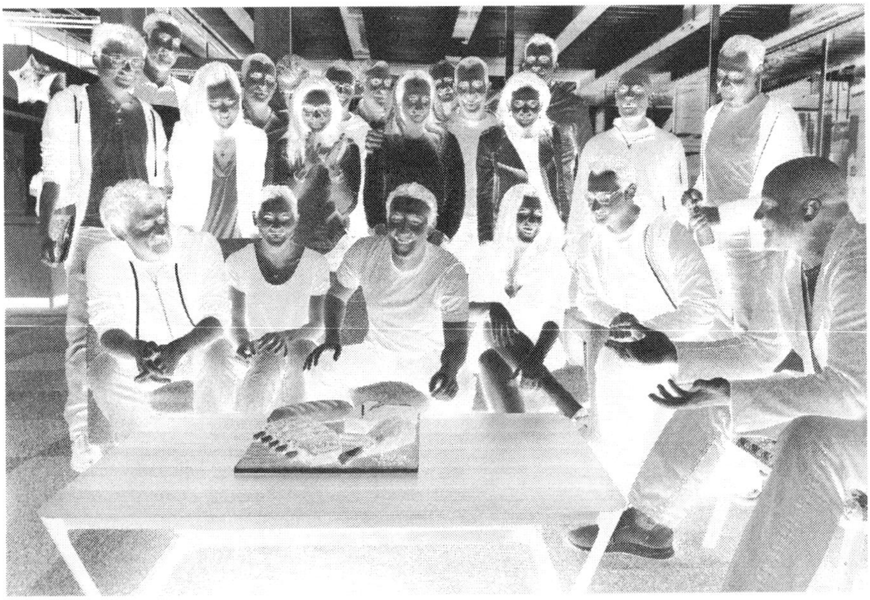

19 PEOPLE, PEOPLE SMILING, PEOPLE SITTING, TABLE AND INDOOR

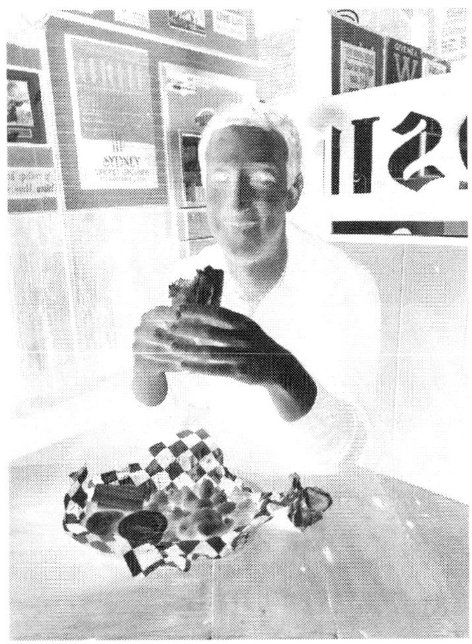
SYDNEY

1 PERSON, FOOD AND INDOOR

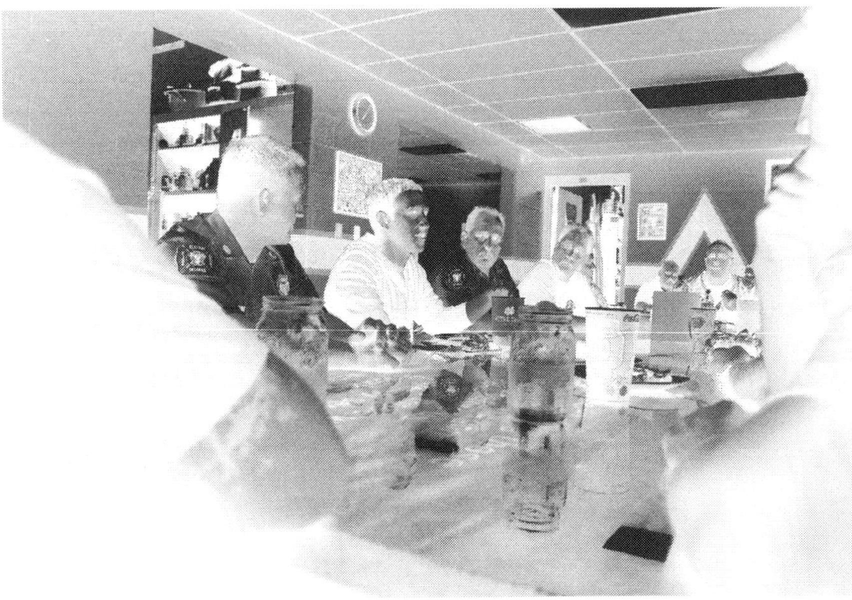

6 PEOPLE, PEOPLE SITTING AND INDOOR

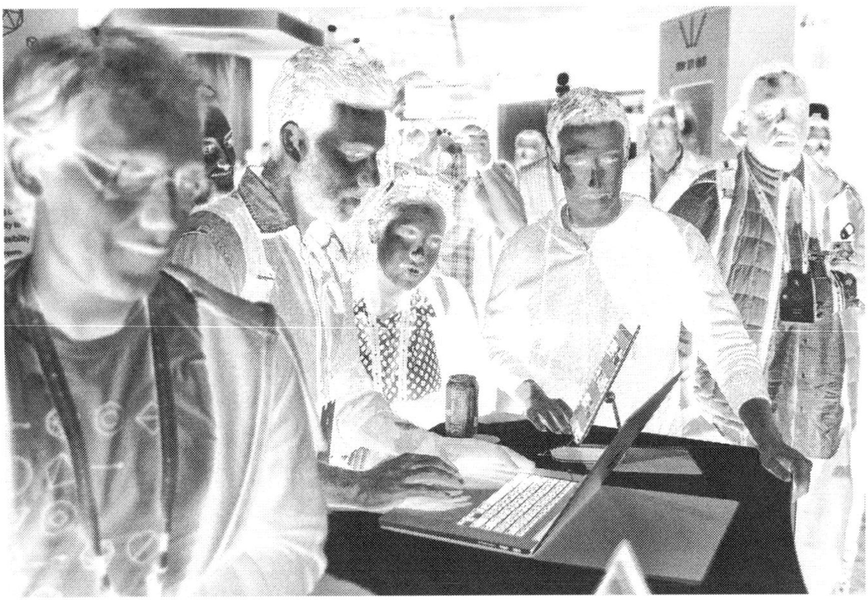

9 PEOPLE, PEOPLE SMILING, PEOPLE SITTING

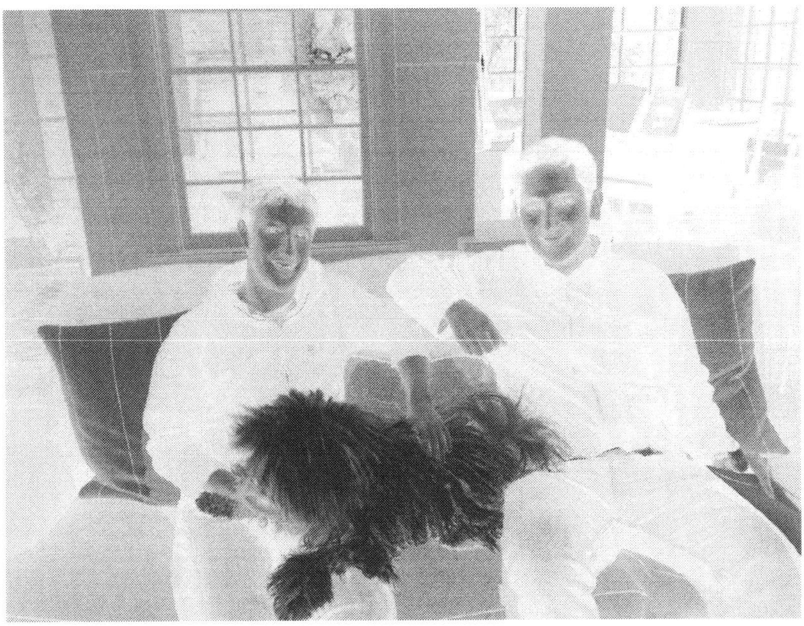

2 PEOPLE, PEOPLE SMILING, PEOPLE
SITTING

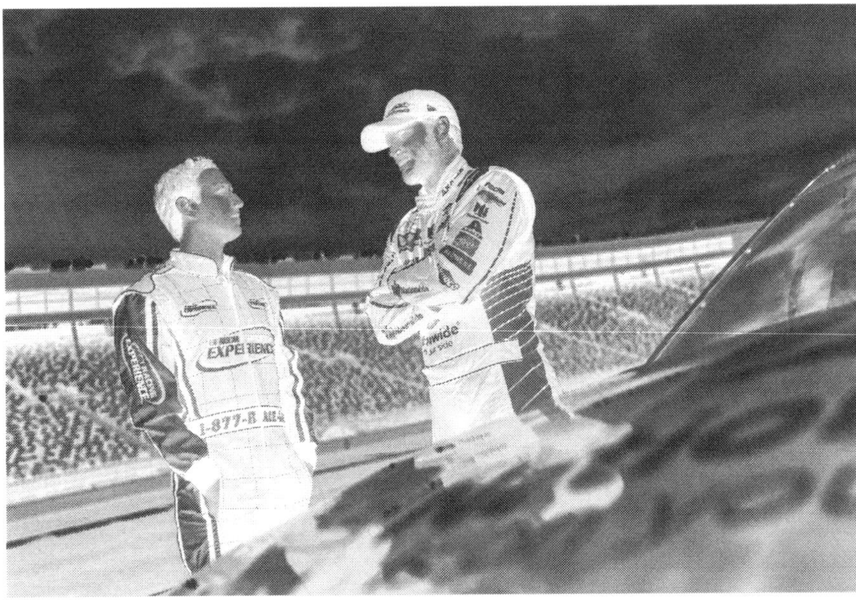

2 PEOPLE, SKY AND OUTDOOR

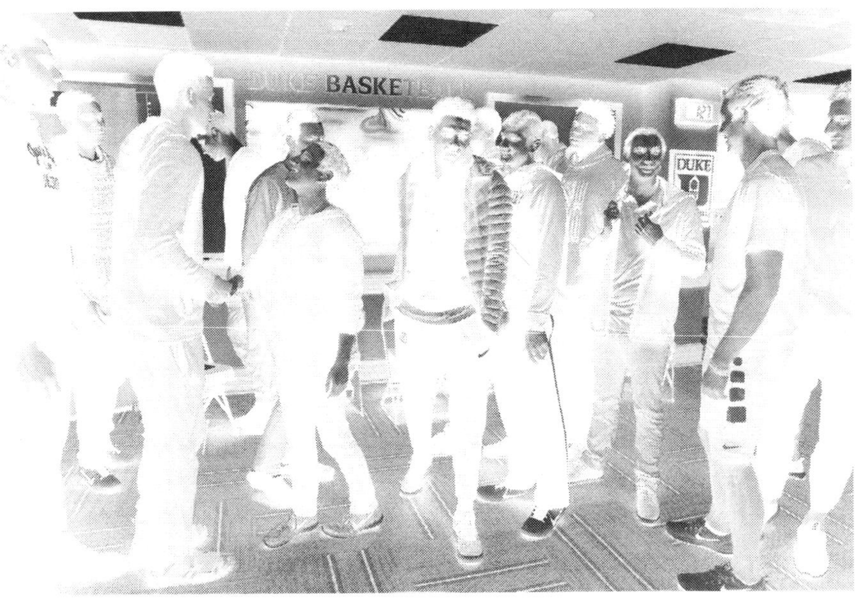
DUKE

8 PEOPLE, PEOPLE SMILING, PEOPLE STANDING

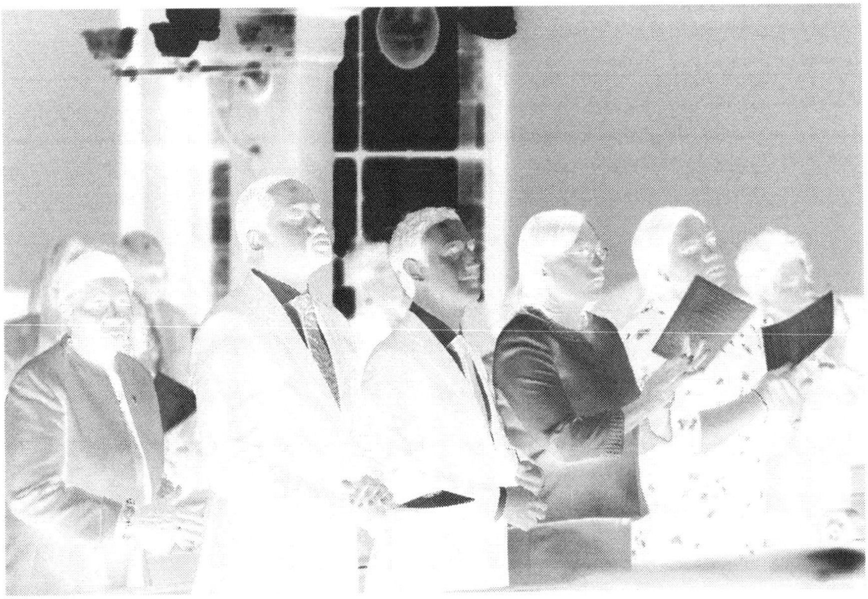

5 PEOPLE, PEOPLE STANDING AND INDOOR

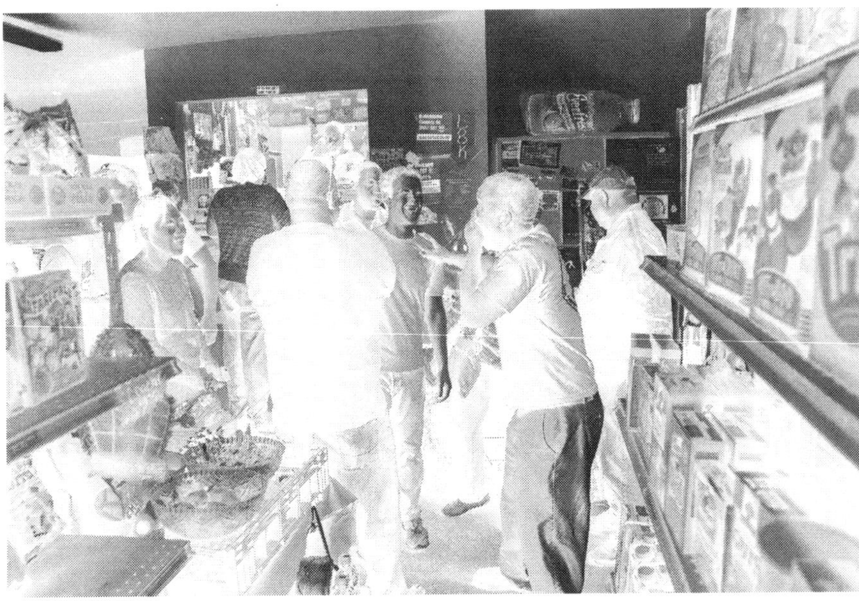

4 PEOPLE, PEOPLE SMILING, PEOPLE STANDING, FOOD AND INDOOR

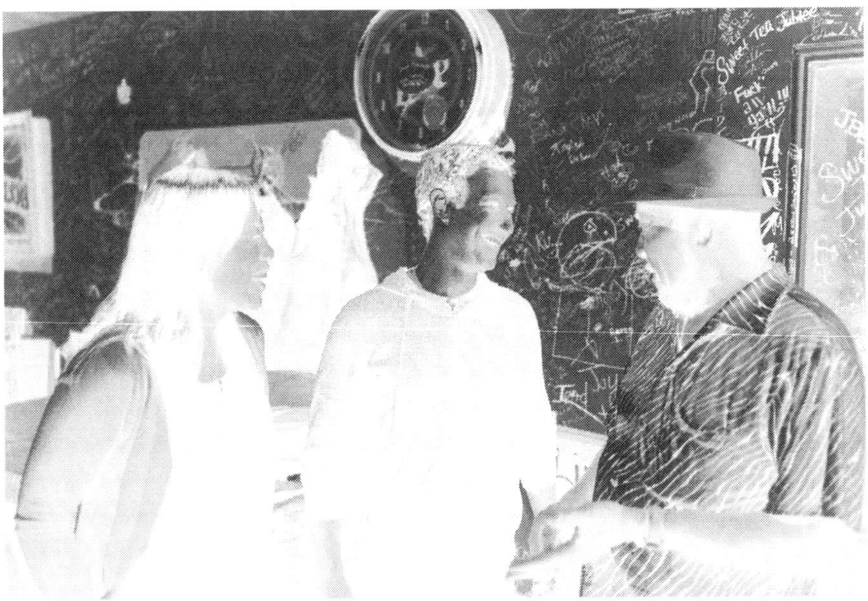
Sweet Tea Jubilee

2 PEOPLE, PEOPLE SMILING, PEOPLE
STANDING AND INDOOR

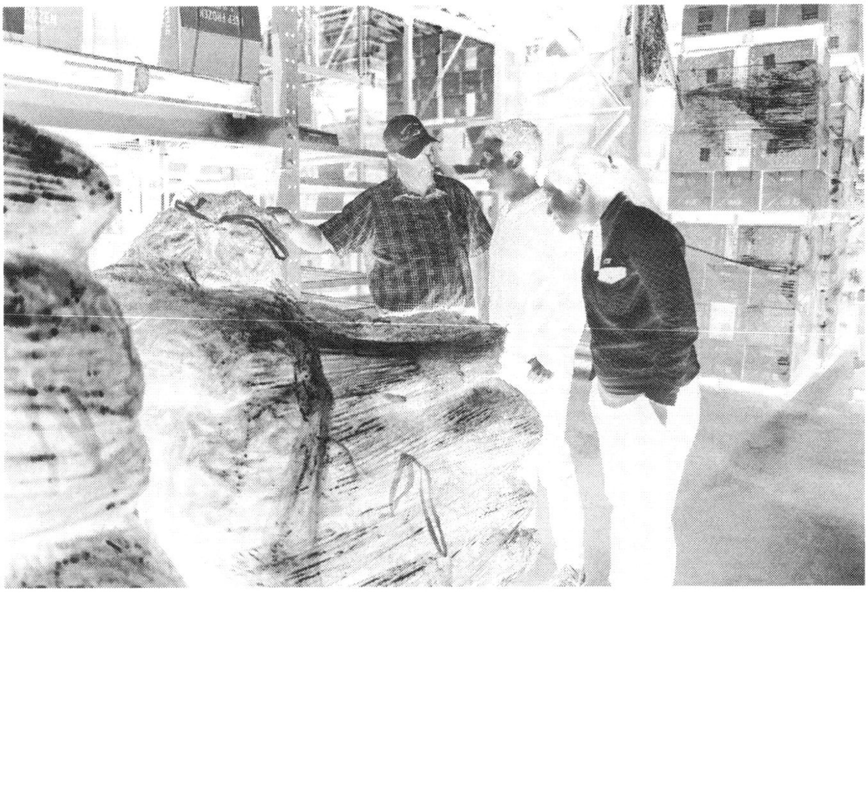

2 PEOPLE, PEOPLE STANDING AND OUTDOOR

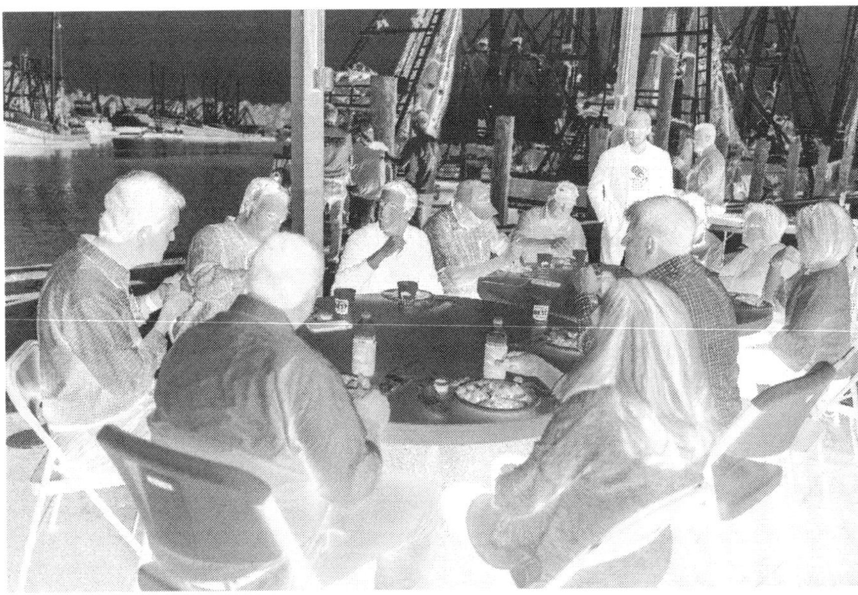

1 PERSON, SITTING, TABLE AND OUTDOOR

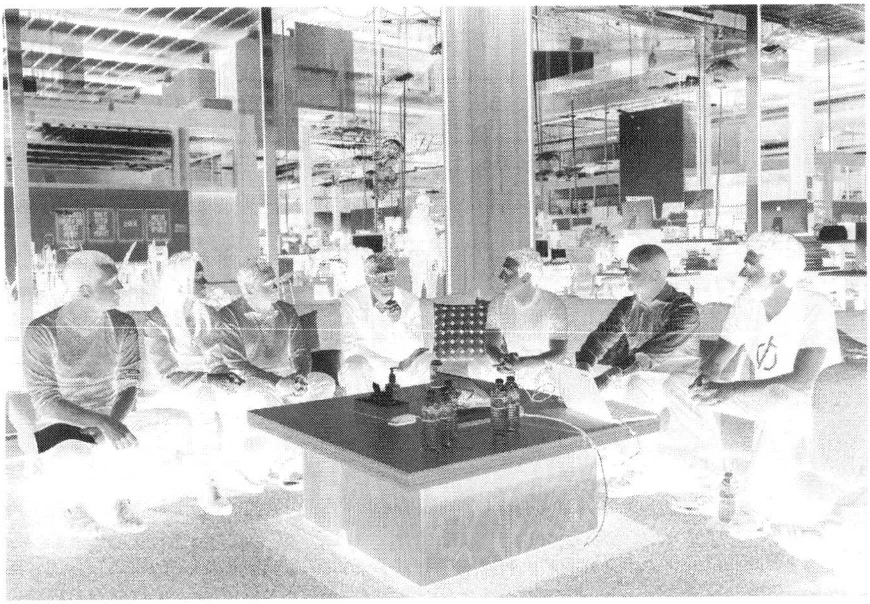

7 PEOPLE, PEOPLE SITTING AND TABLE

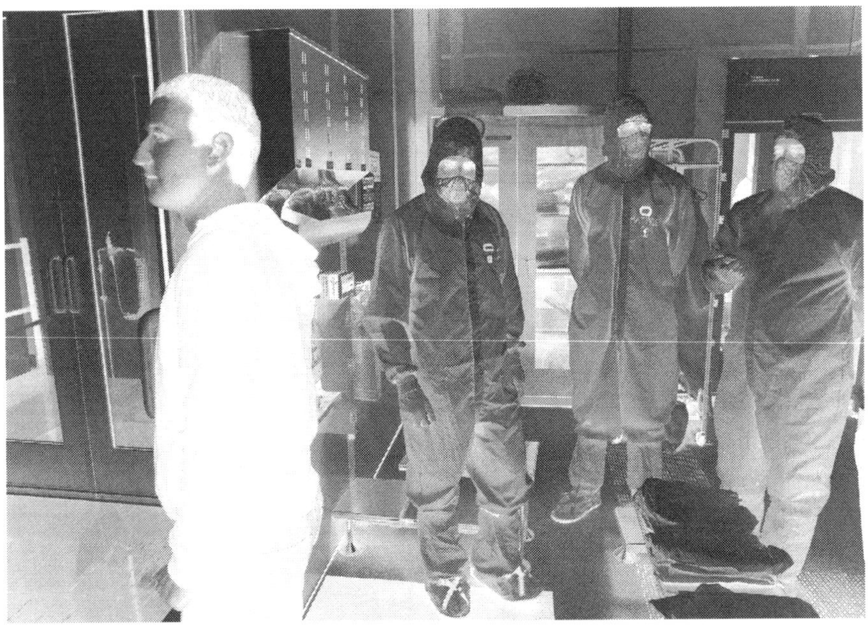

1 PERSON, STANDING AND INDOOR

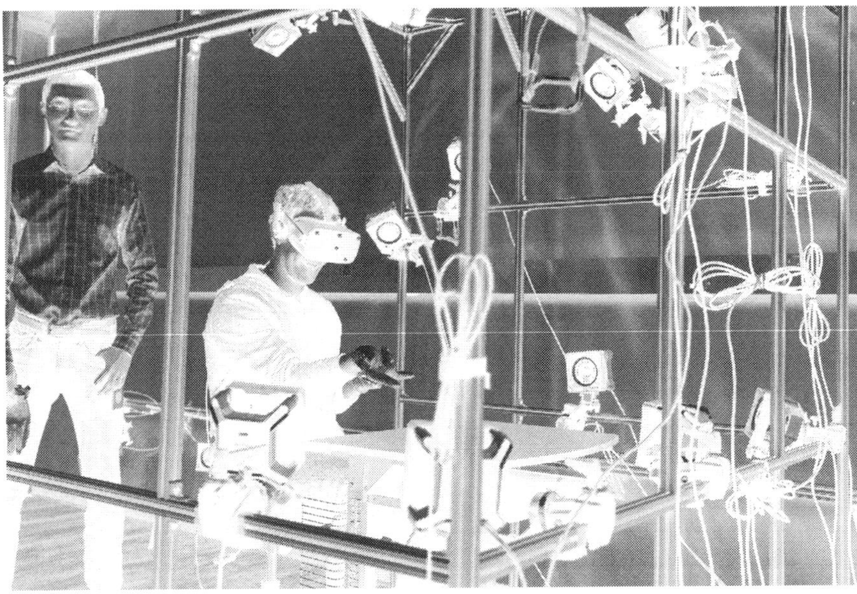

1 PERSON

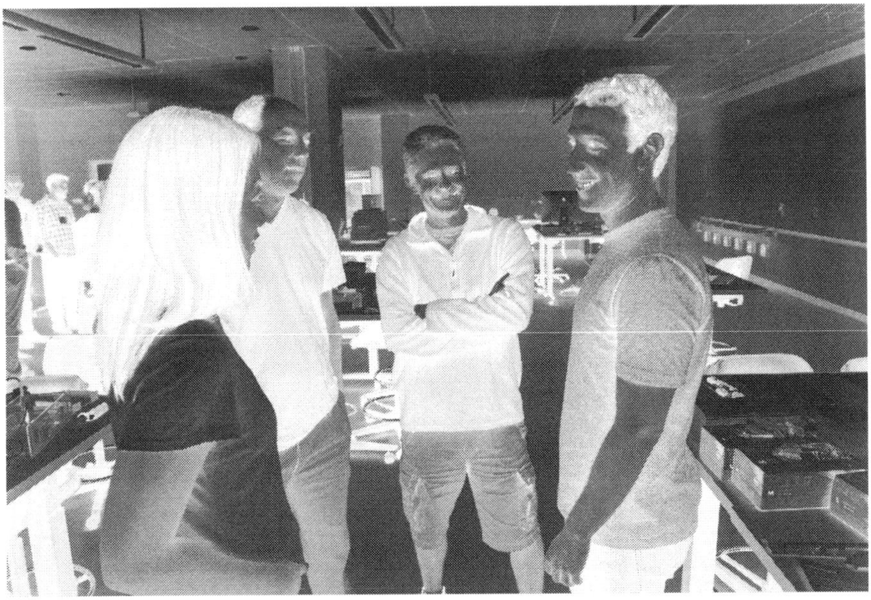

3 PEOPLE, PEOPLE SMILING, PEOPLE STANDING AND INDOOR

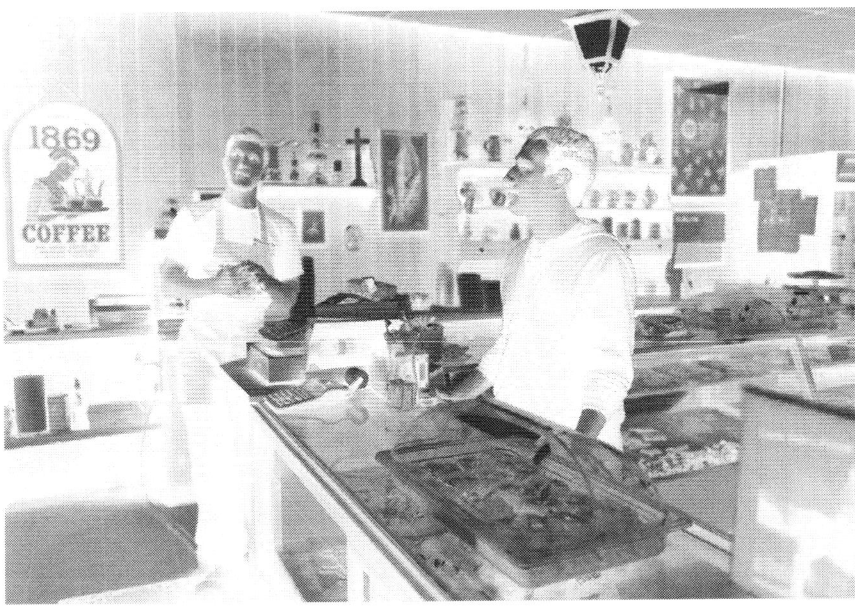
1869
COFFEE

2 PEOPLE, PEOPLE SITTING, PEOPLE EATING, TABLE, INDOOR AND FOOD

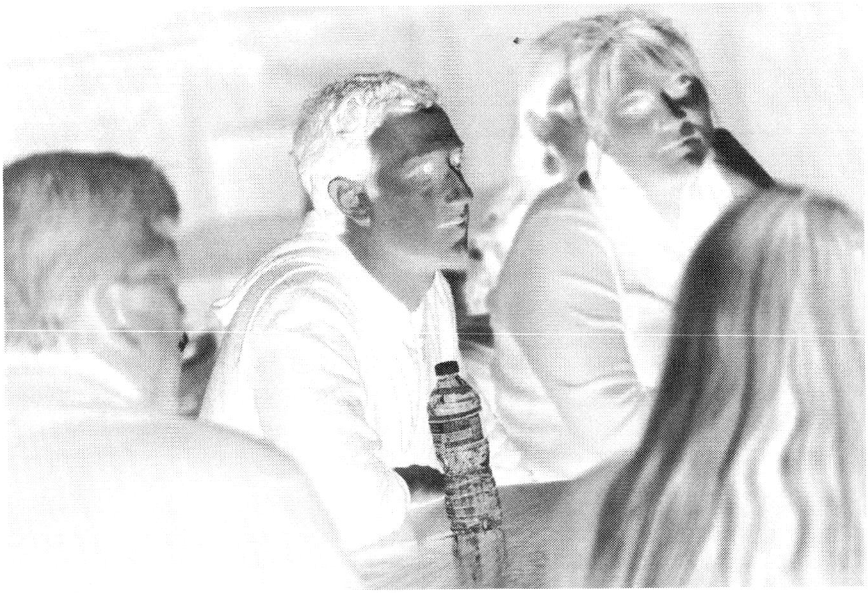

2 PEOPLE, INDOOR

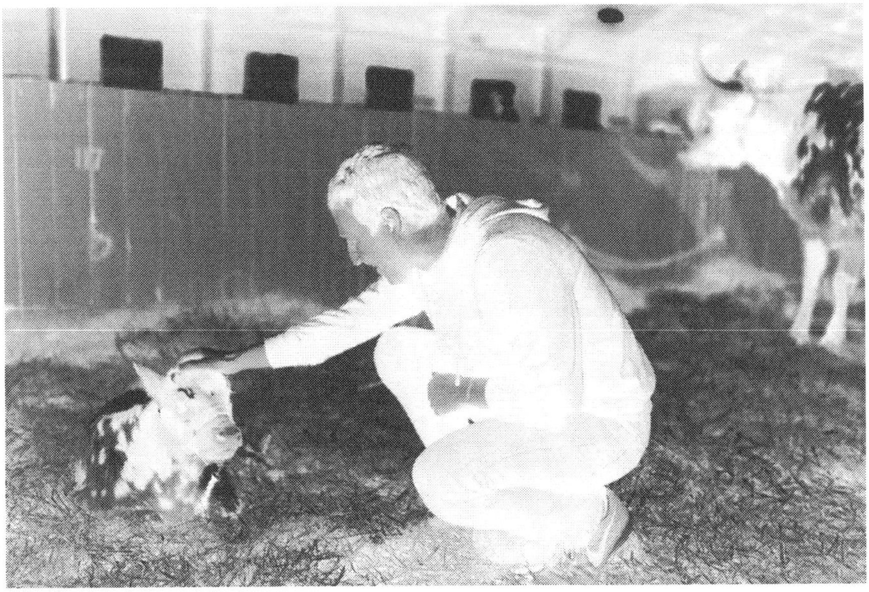

ONE OR MORE PEOPLE AND OUTDOOR

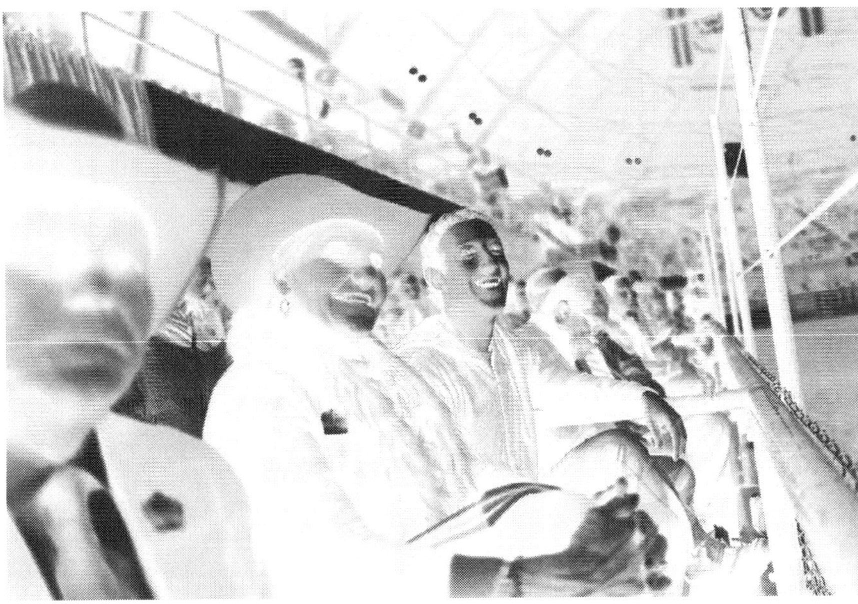

3 PEOPLE, PEOPLE SMILING, HAT

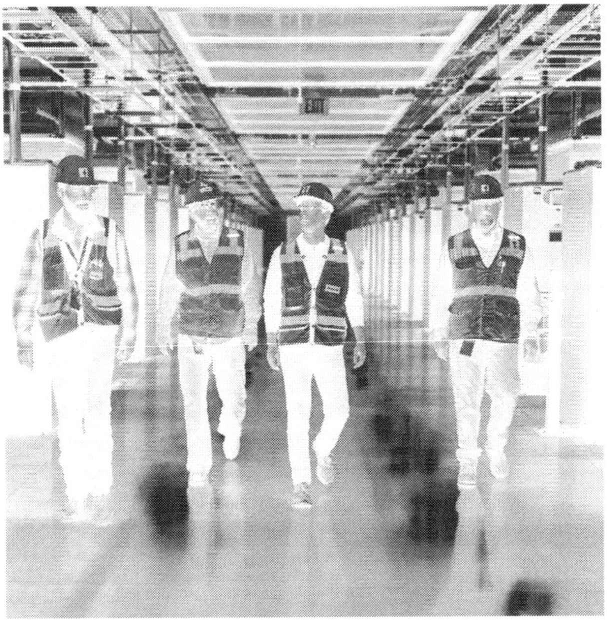

2 PEOPLE, PEOPLE STANDING AND INDOOR

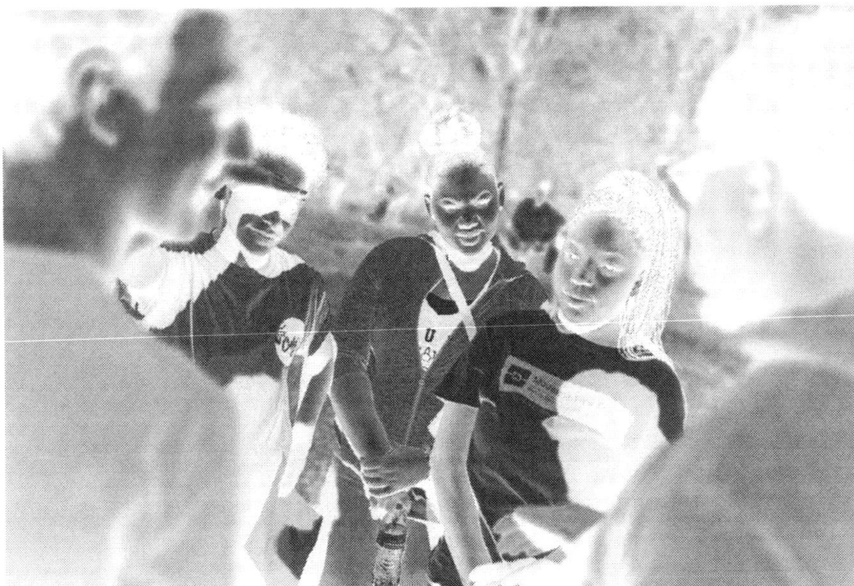

4 PEOPLE, PEOPLE SITTING AND OUTDOOR

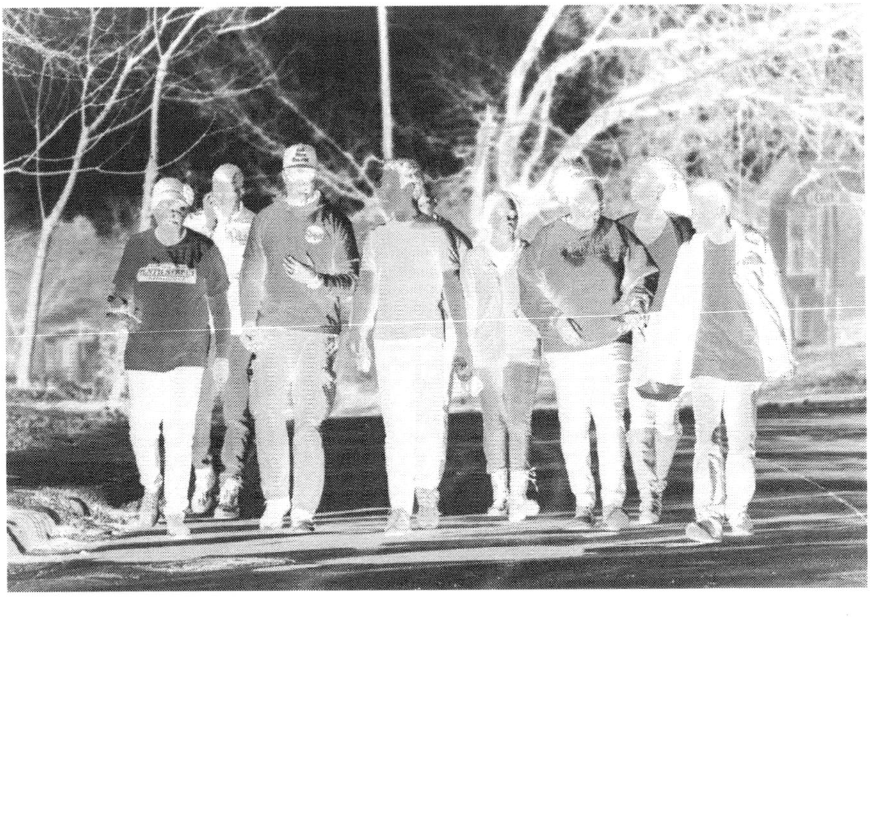

3 PEOPLE, PEOPLE SMILING, PEOPLE STANDING, SHOES, TREE, SKY, CHILD AND OUTDOOR

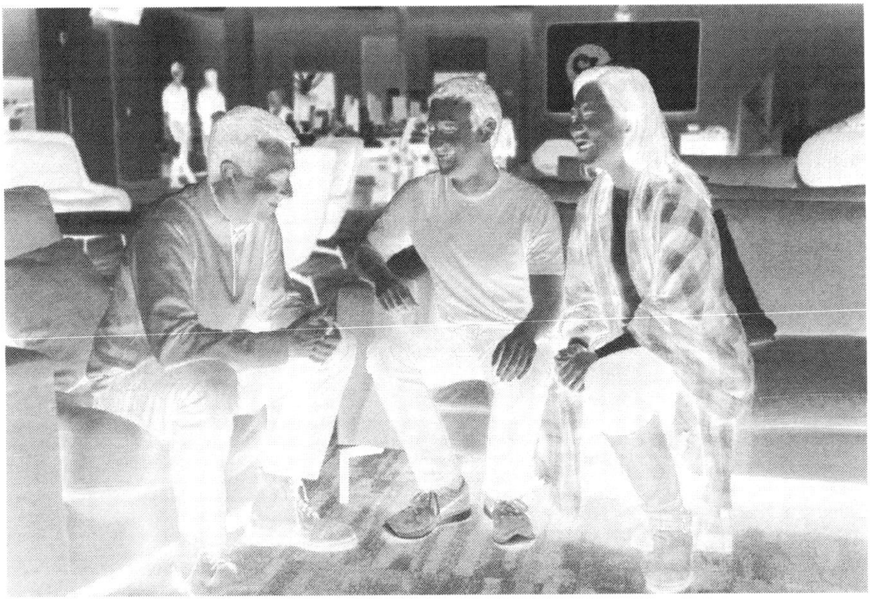

3 PEOPLE, PEOPLE SMILING, PEOPLE SITTING AND LIVING ROOM

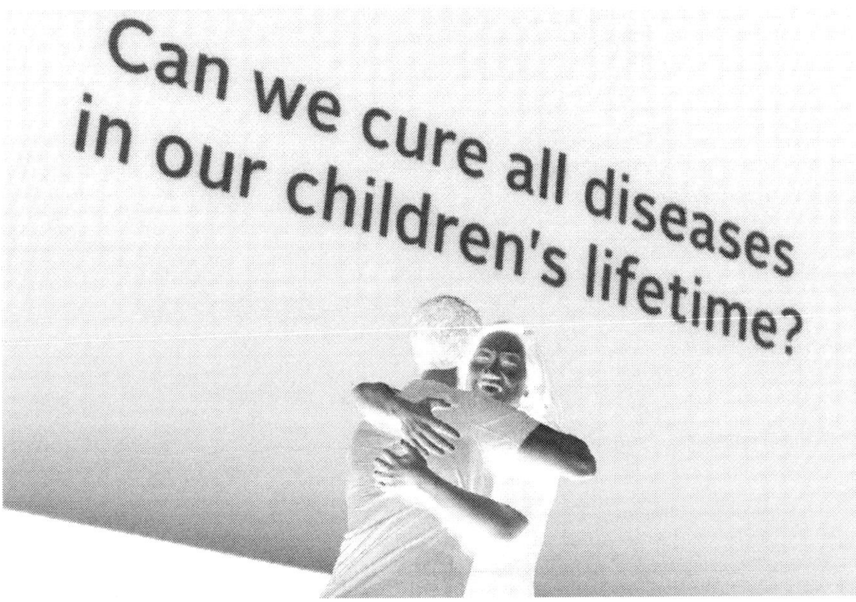
Can we cure all diseases
in our children's lifetime?

1 PERSON, SMILING, TEXT

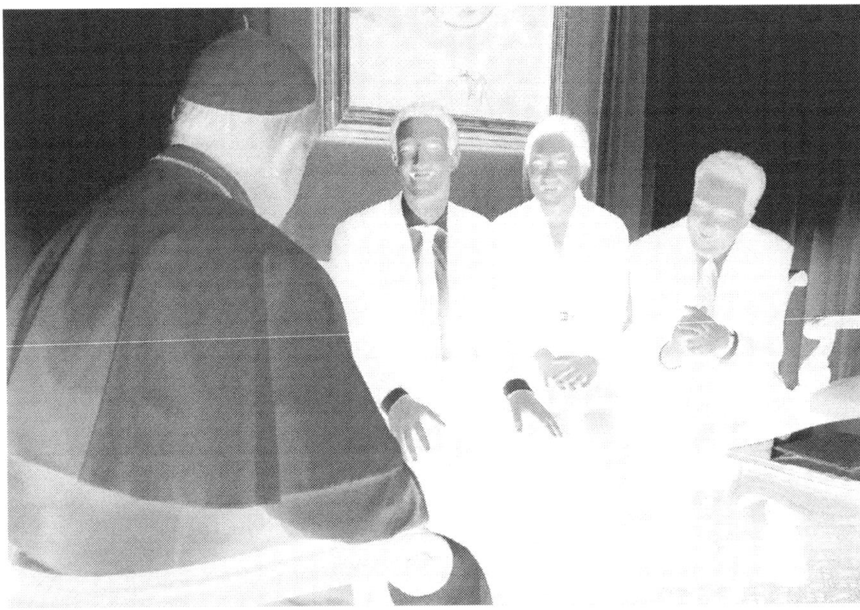

3 PEOPLE, PEOPLE SMILING, PEOPLE SITTING

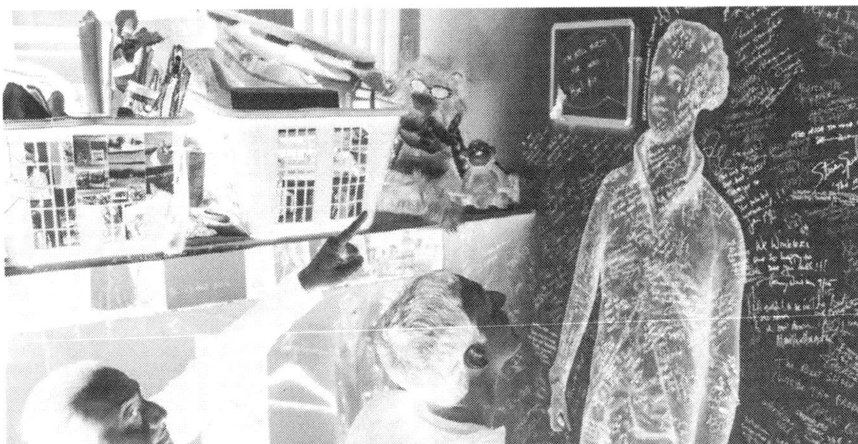

2 PEOPLE, PEOPLE STANDING

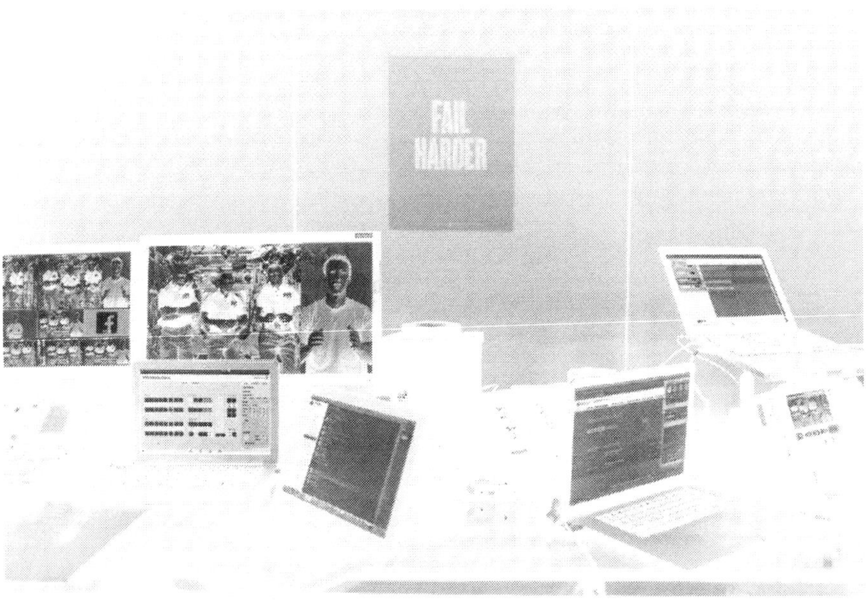
FAIL
HARDER

1 PERSON, SCREEN

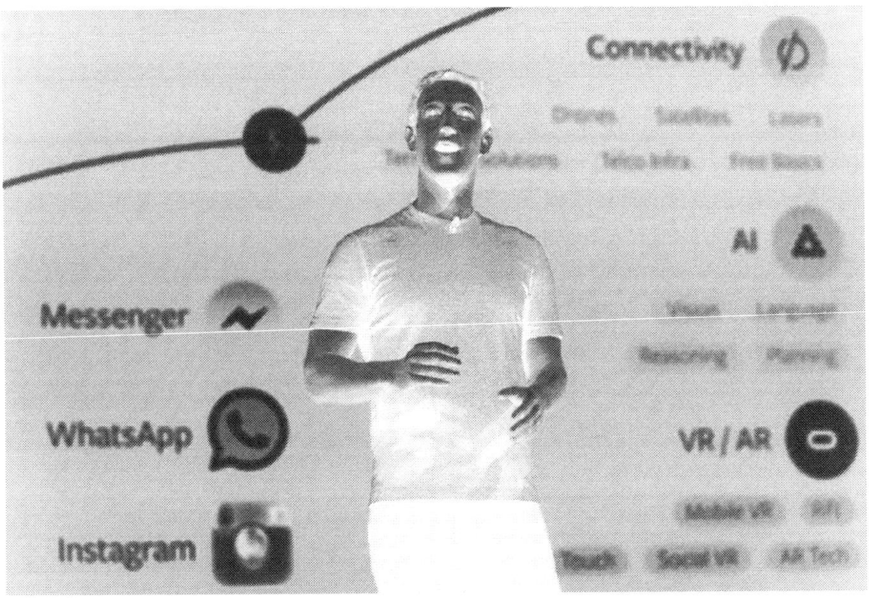
Connectivity
AI
Messenger
WhatsApp
VR / AR
Instagram

1 PERSON, STANDING AND TEXT

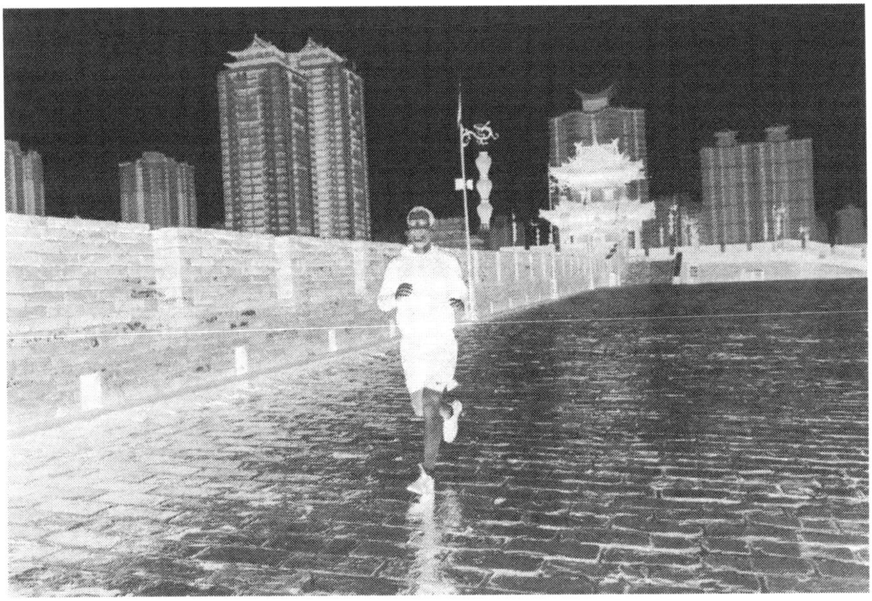

1 PERSON, SMILING, STANDING, SHOES, SKY, OUTDOOR AND WATER

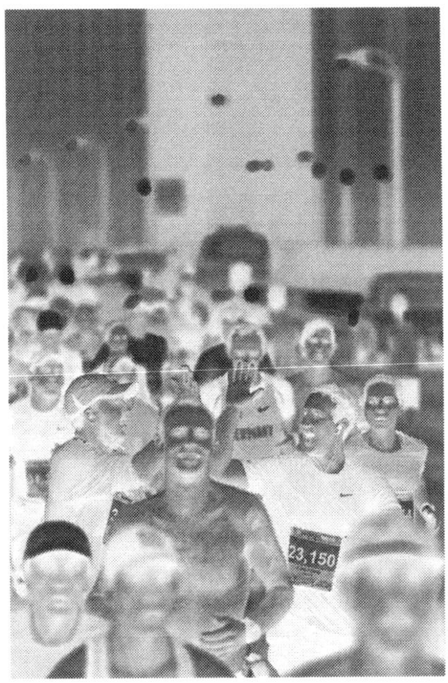
23,150

6 PEOPLE, PEOPLE SMILING, OUTDOOR AND INDOOR

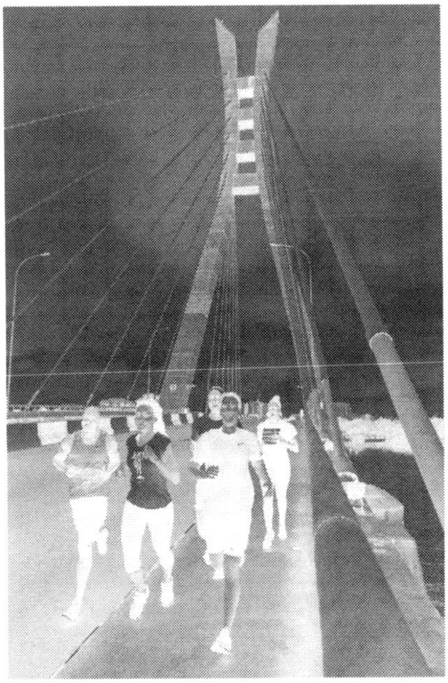

3 PEOPLE, PEOPLE SMILING, PEOPLE STANDING, SKY, BRIDGE, CLOUD AND OUTDOOR

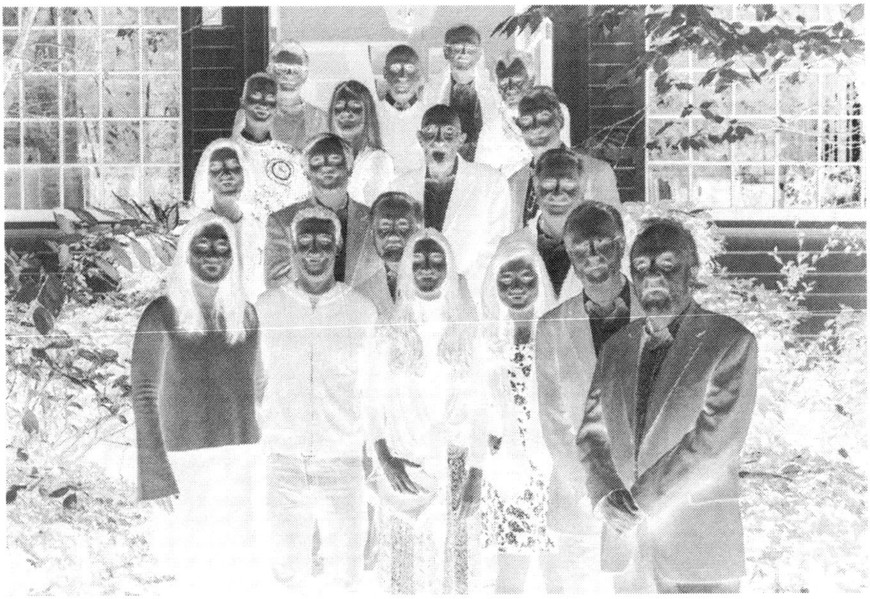

18 PEOPLE, PEOPLE SMILING, PEOPLE STANDING

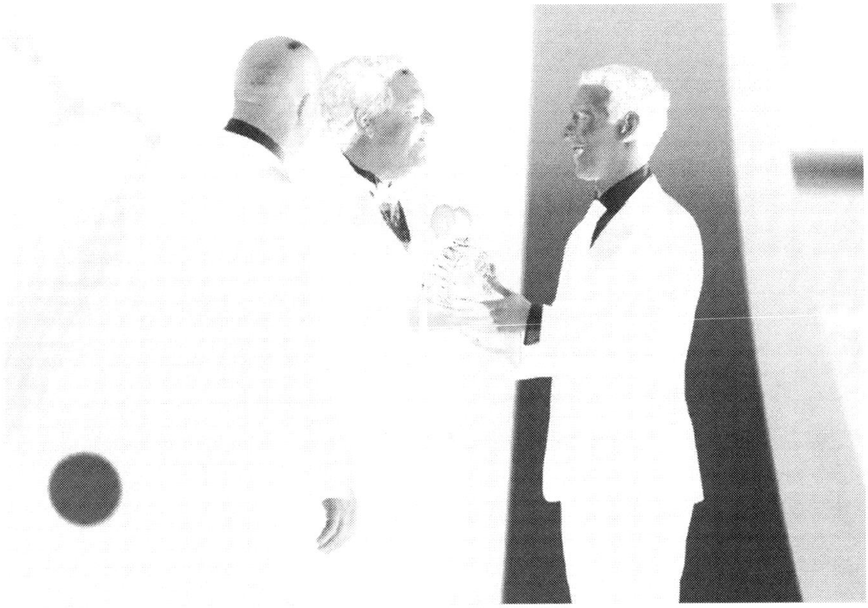

2 PEOPLE, PEOPLE STANDING AND SUIT

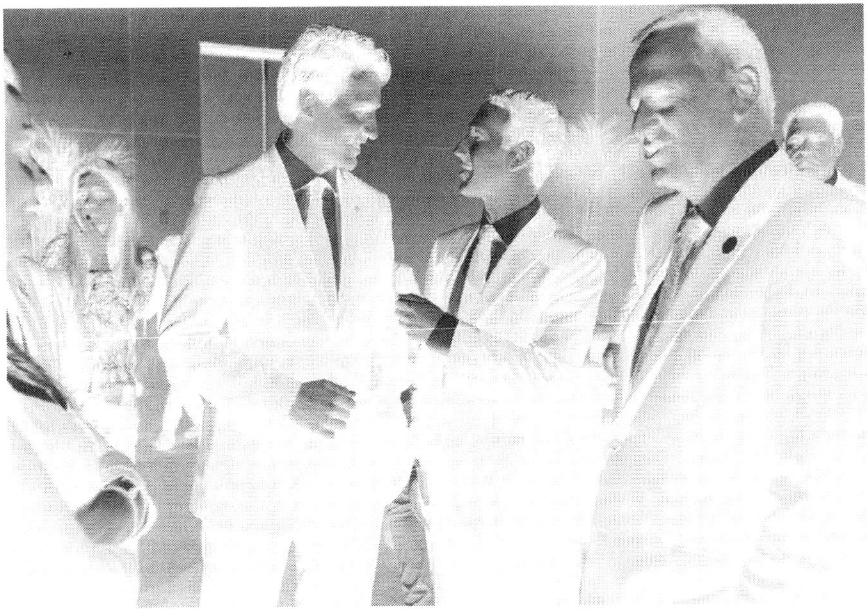

5 PEOPLE, SUIT

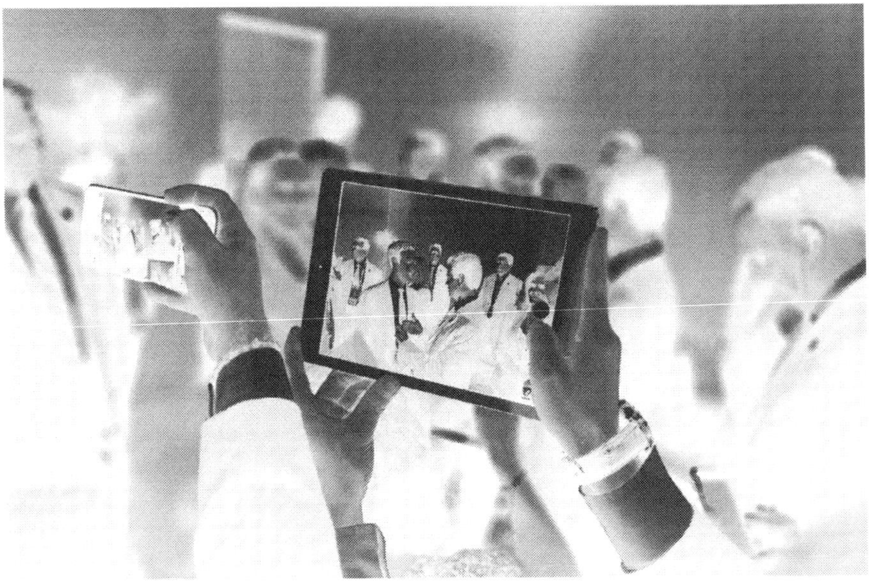

2 PEOPLE, PHONE AND SCREEN

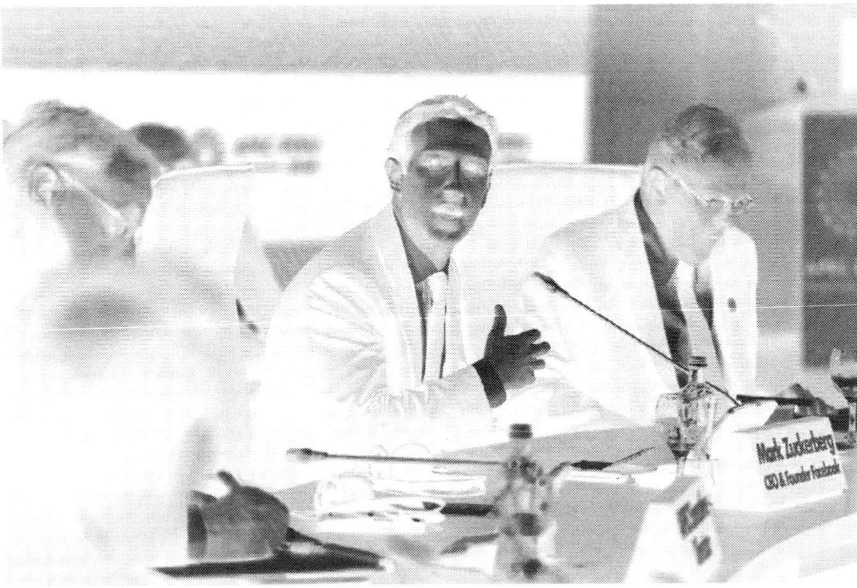
Mark Zuckerberg
CEO & Founder Facebook

1 PERSON, SITTING

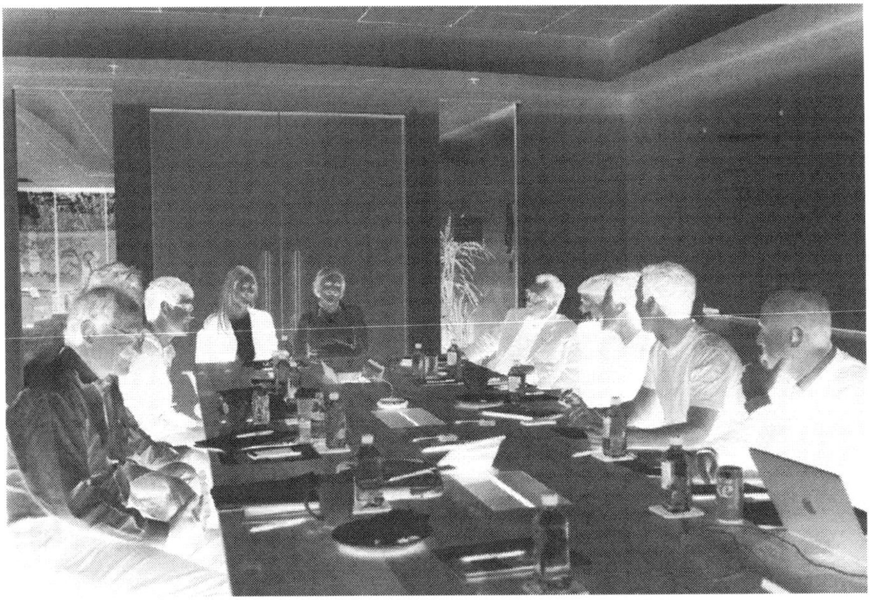

4 PEOPLE, PEOPLE SMILING, PEOPLE SITTING, TABLE AND INDOOR

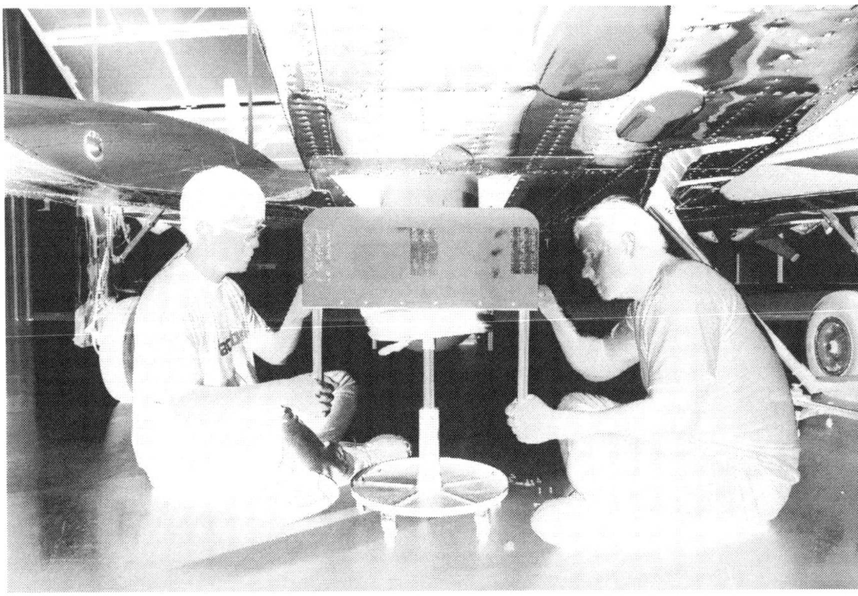

1 PERSON, SITTING

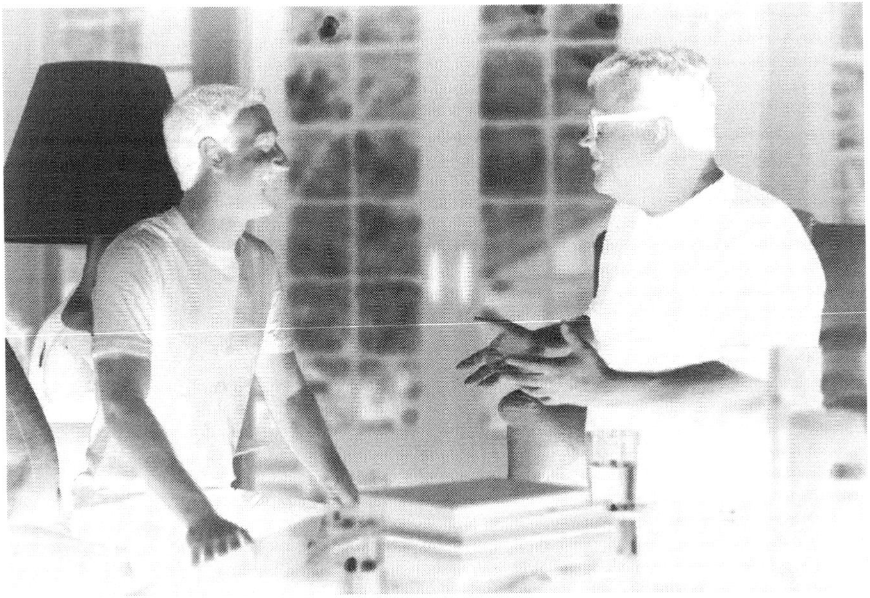

2 PEOPLE, PEOPLE SITTING, TABLE AND INDOOR

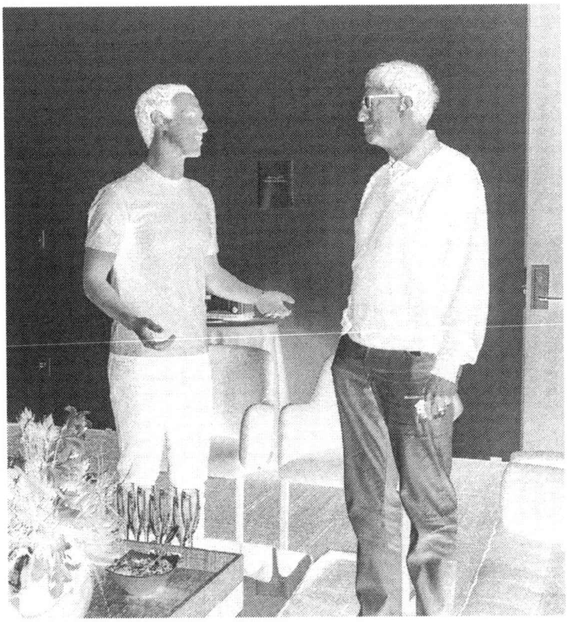

ONE OR MORE PEOPLE, PEOPLE STANDING,
SHOES AND INDOOR

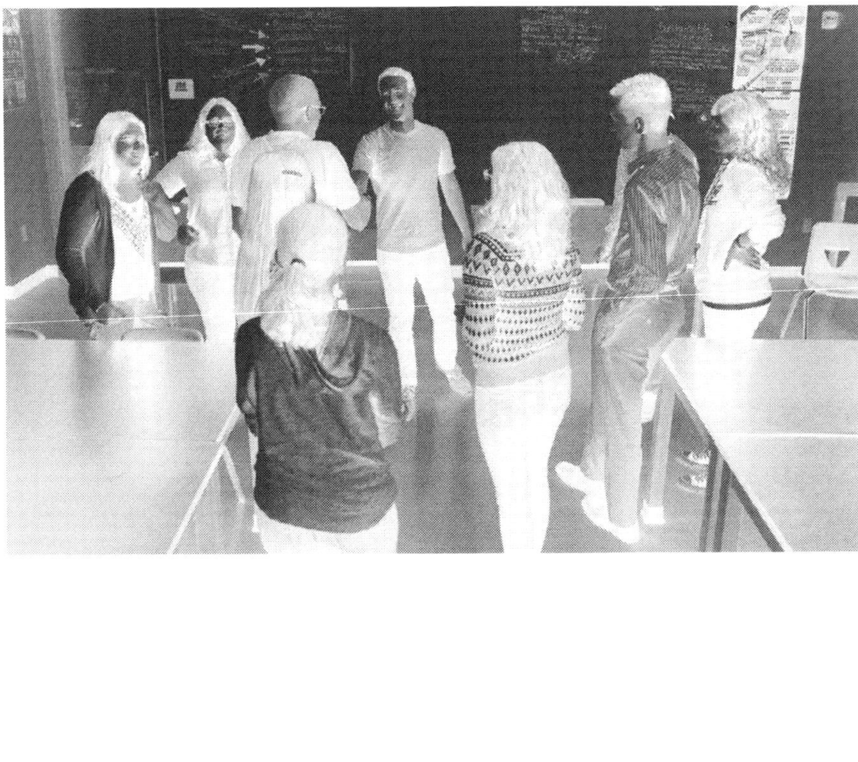

4 PEOPLE, PEOPLE SMILING, PEOPLE STANDING AND INDOOR

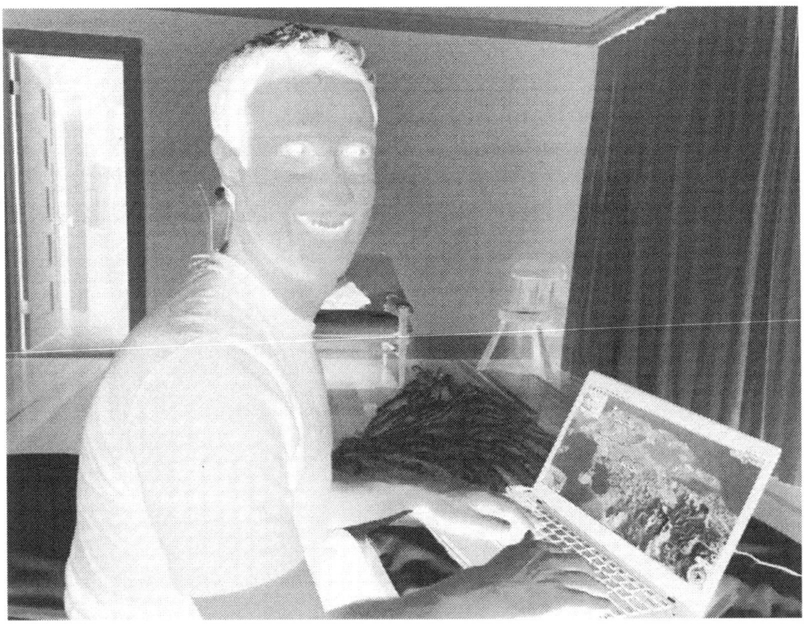

1 PERSON, SMILING, SITTING, LAPTOP,
PHONE AND INDOOR

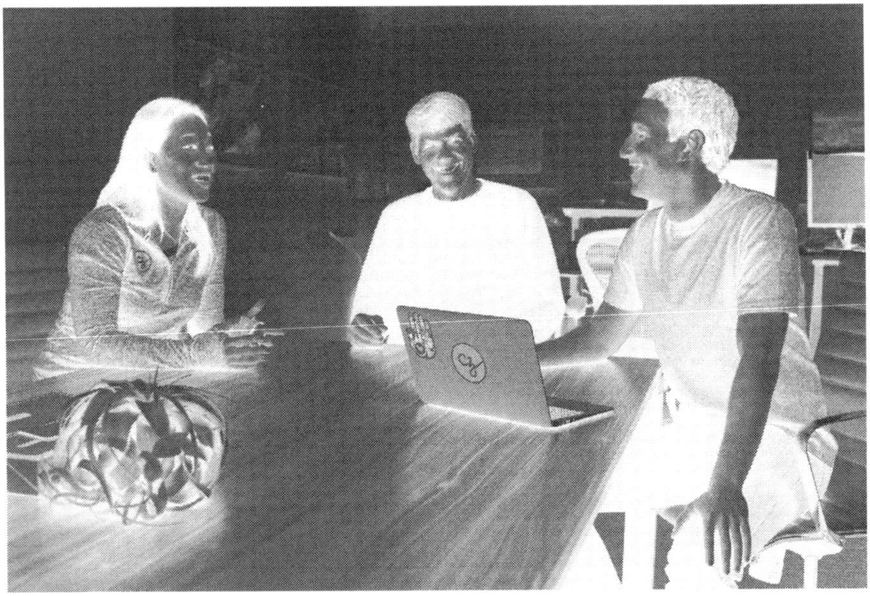

3 PEOPLE, PEOPLE SMILING, PEOPLE SITTING AND INDOOR

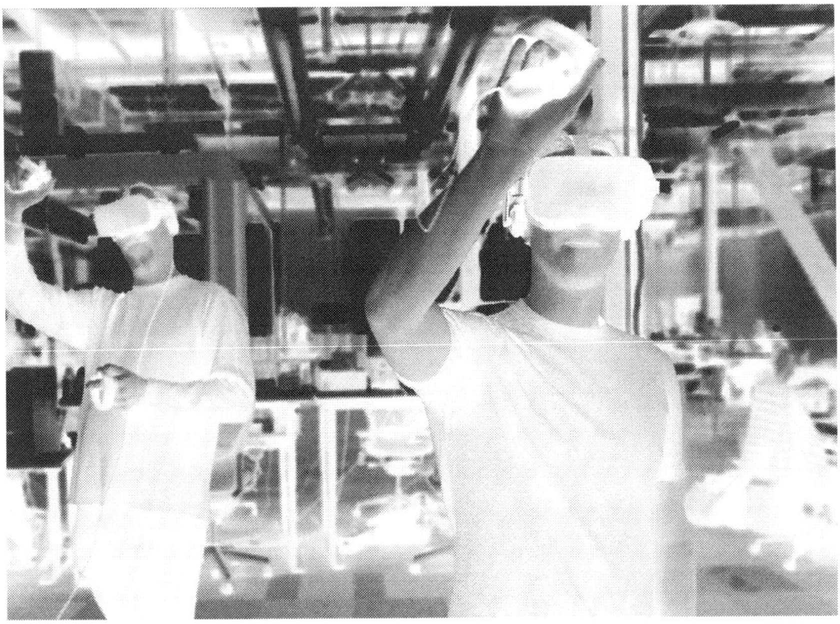

ONE OR MORE PEOPLE, PEOPLE STANDING,
PHONE, SUNGLASSES AND CLOSEUP

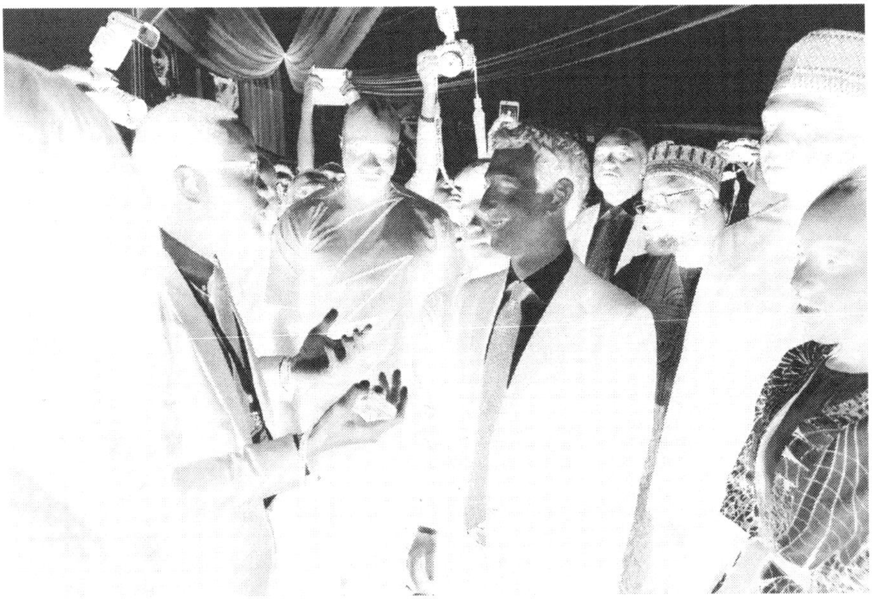

6 PEOPLE, PEOPLE STANDING AND SUIT

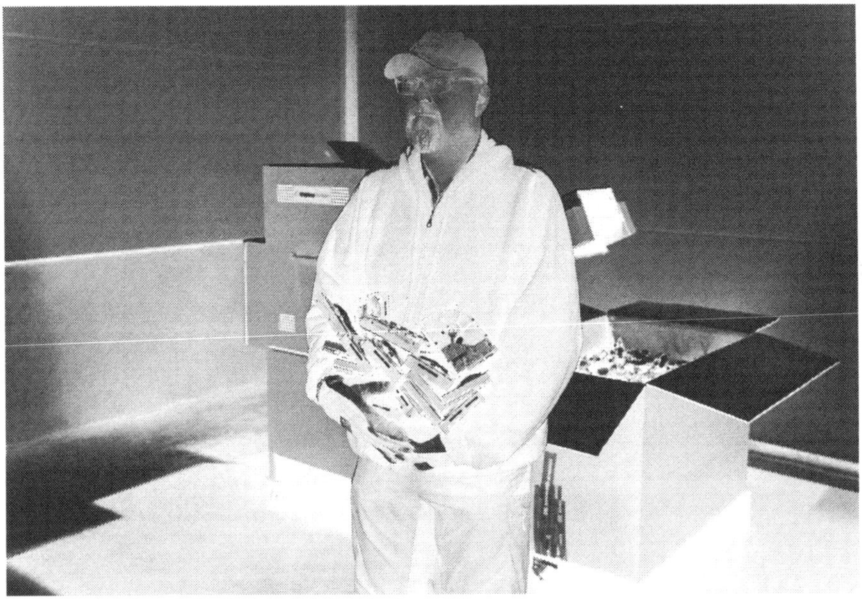

ONE OR MORE PEOPLE AND INDOOR

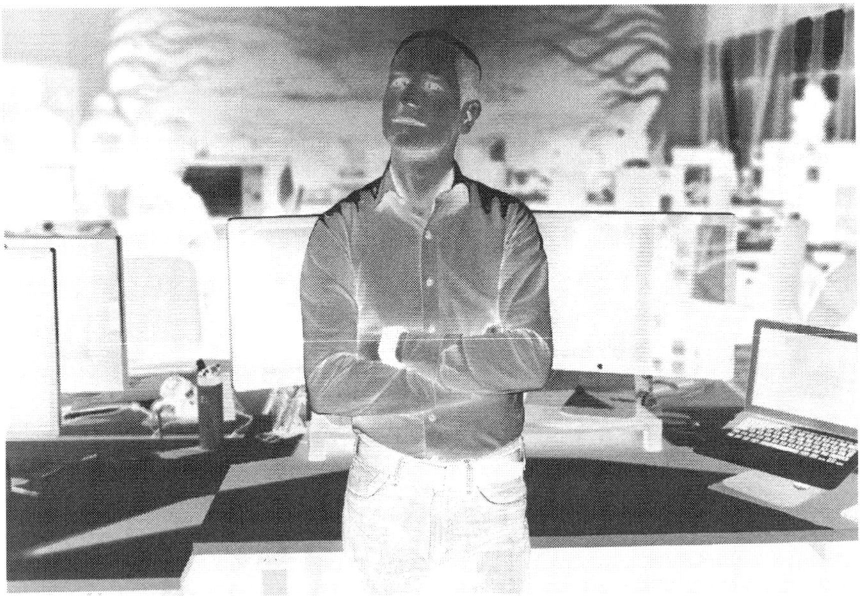

1 PERSON, INDOOR

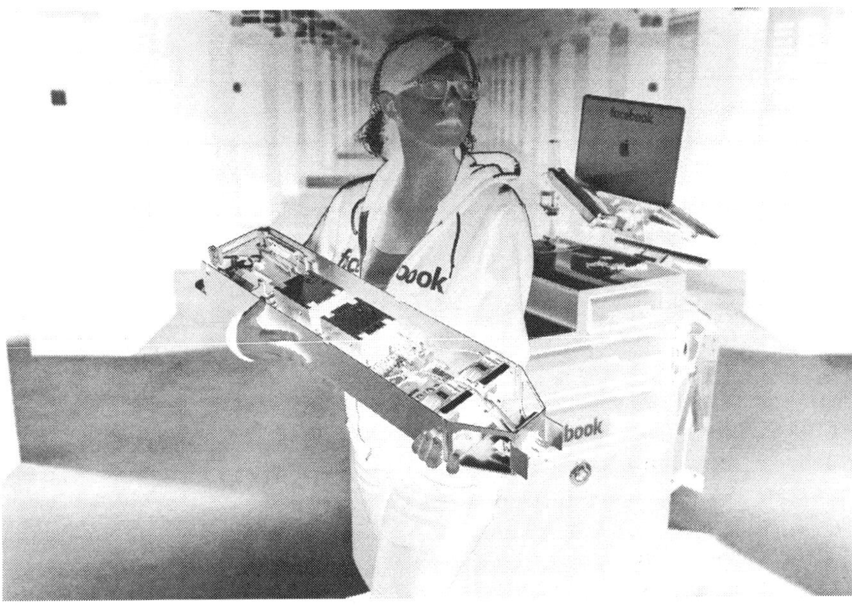

1 PERSON, SCREEN AND INDOOR

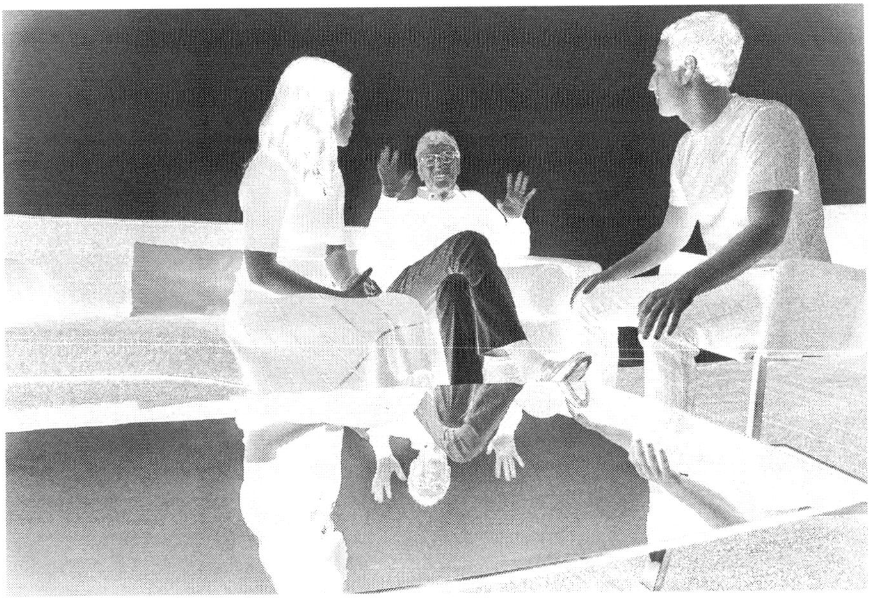

1 PERSON, SITTING

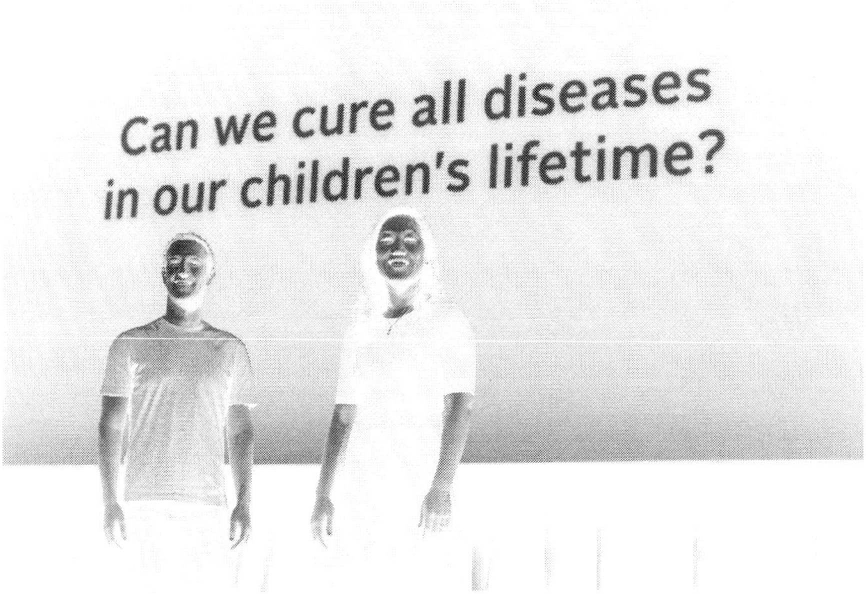
Can we cure all diseases
in our children's lifetime?

2 PEOPLE, PEOPLE SMILING, PEOPLE
STANDING AND TEXT

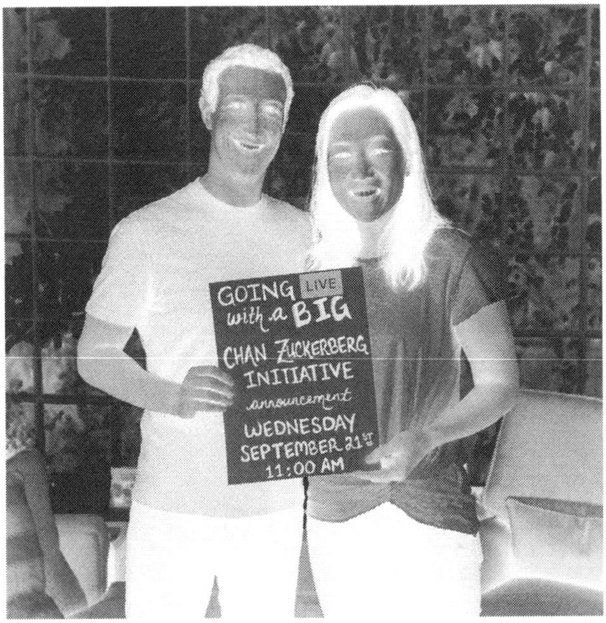
GOING LIVE
with a BIG
CHAN ZUCKERBERG
INITIATIVE
announcement
WEDNESDAY
SEPTEMBER 21ST
11:00 AM

2 PEOPLE, PEOPLE SMILING

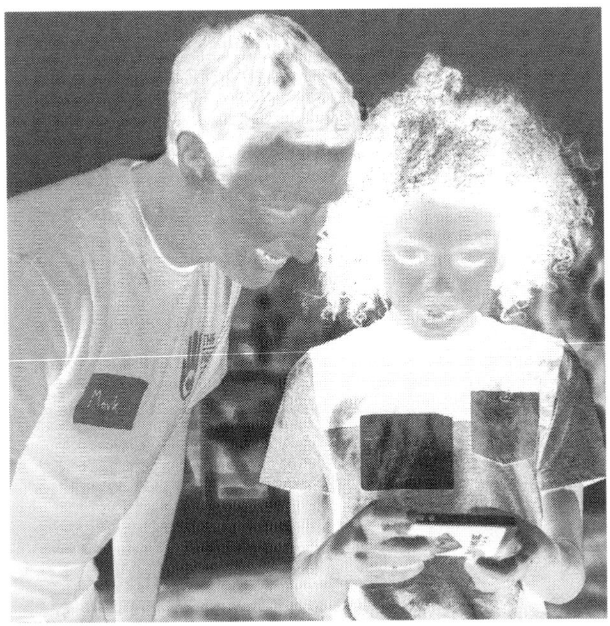
Mark

1 PERSON, CHILD AND OUTDOOR

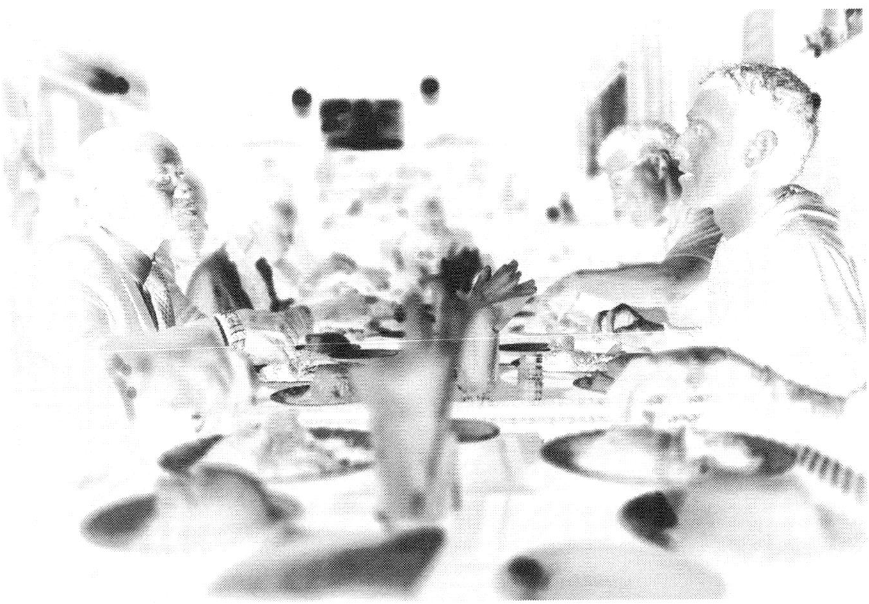

2 PEOPLE, PEOPLE EATING, PEOPLE
SITTING, TABLE, FOOD AND INDOOR

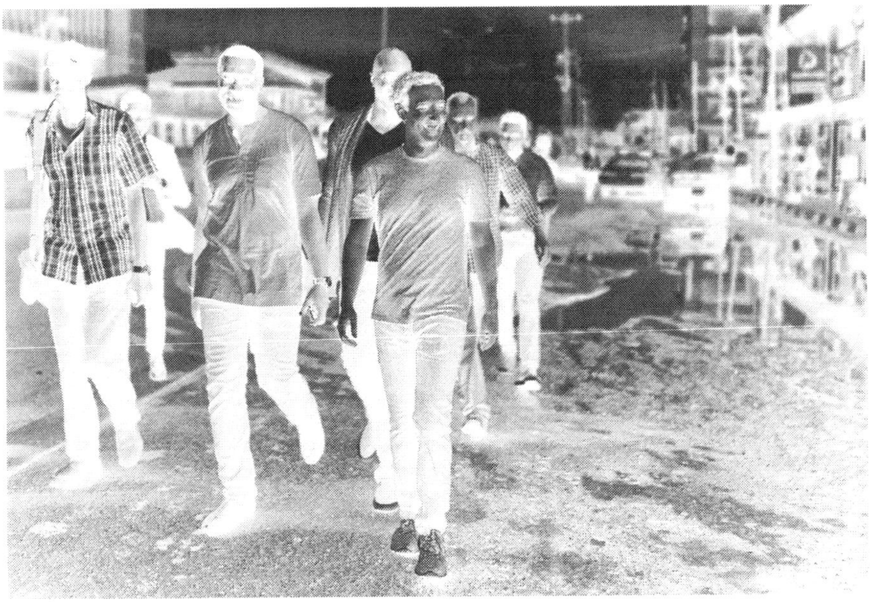

3 PEOPLE, PEOPLE SMILING, PEOPLE STANDING, PEOPLE WALKING AND OUTDOOR

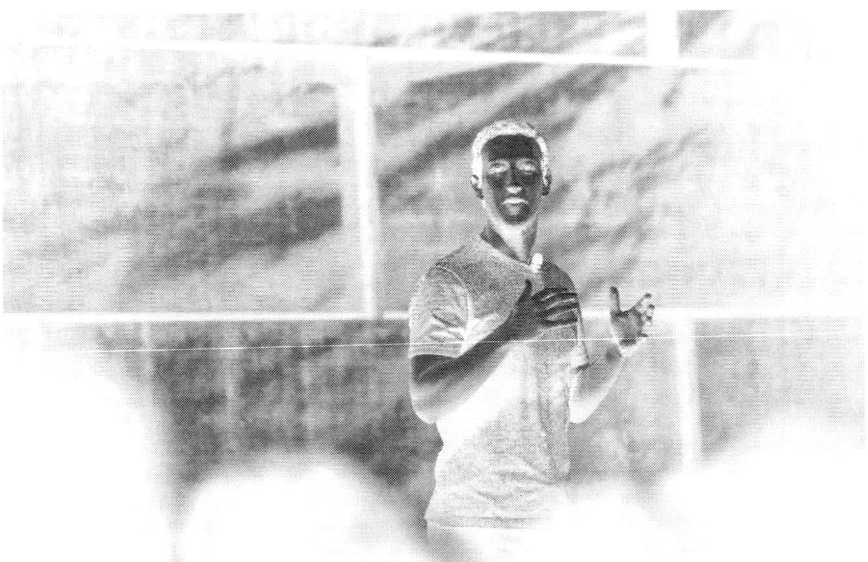

1 PERSON

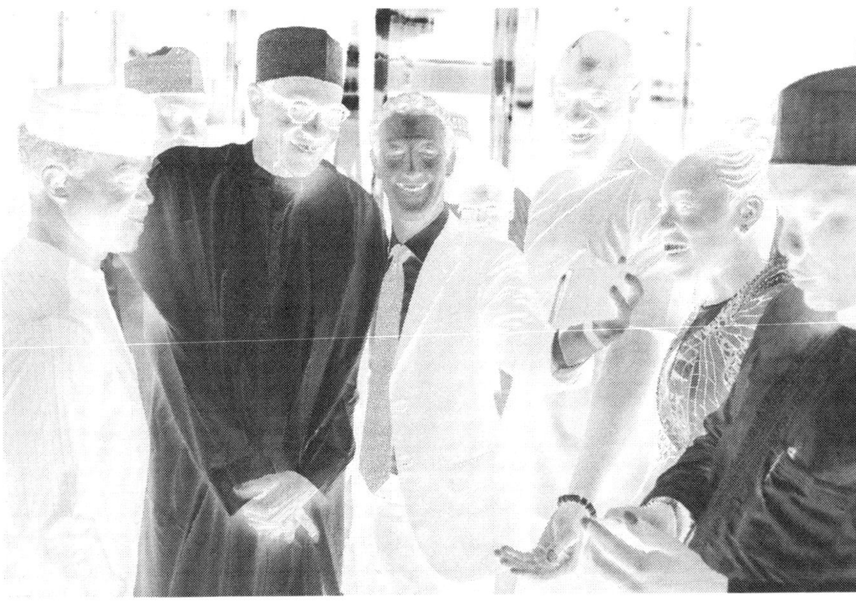

6 PEOPLE, PEOPLE SMILING

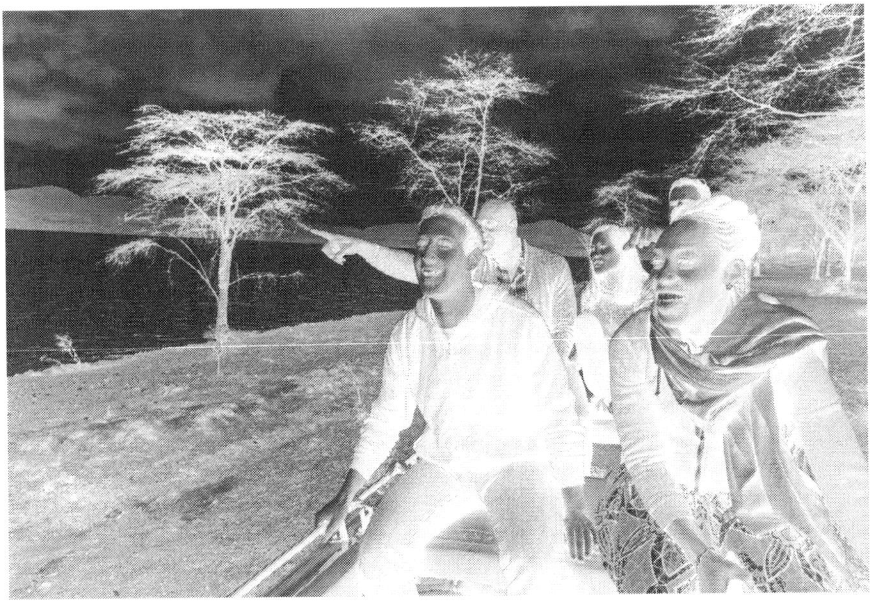

4 PEOPLE, PEOPLE SMILING, SKY, TREE, CLOUD, OUTDOOR AND NATURE

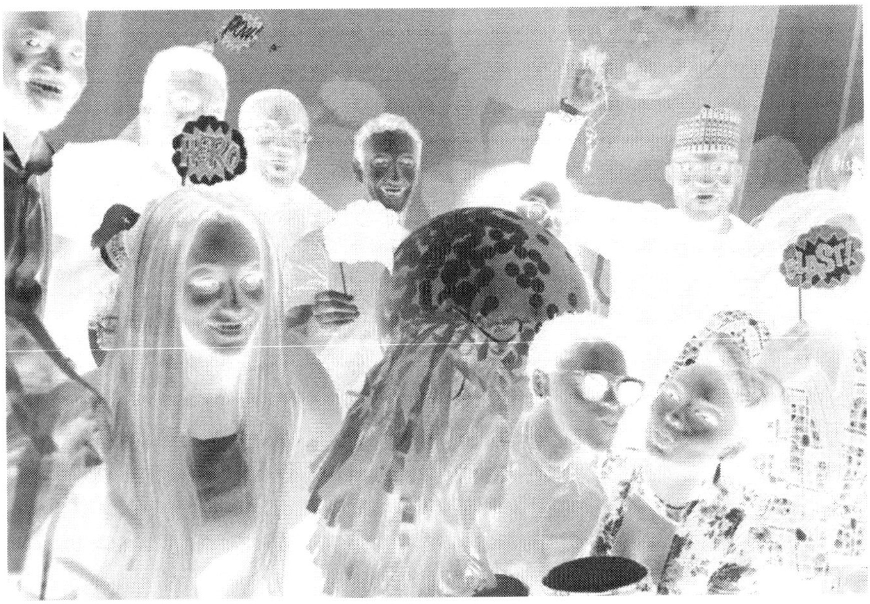

8 PEOPLE, PEOPLE SMILING, PEOPLE STANDING

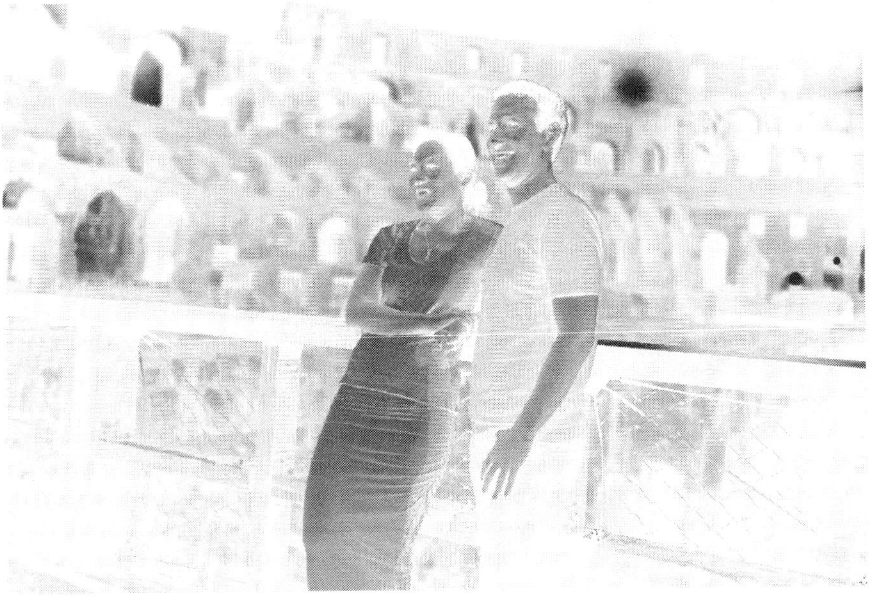

2 PEOPLE, PEOPLE STANDING

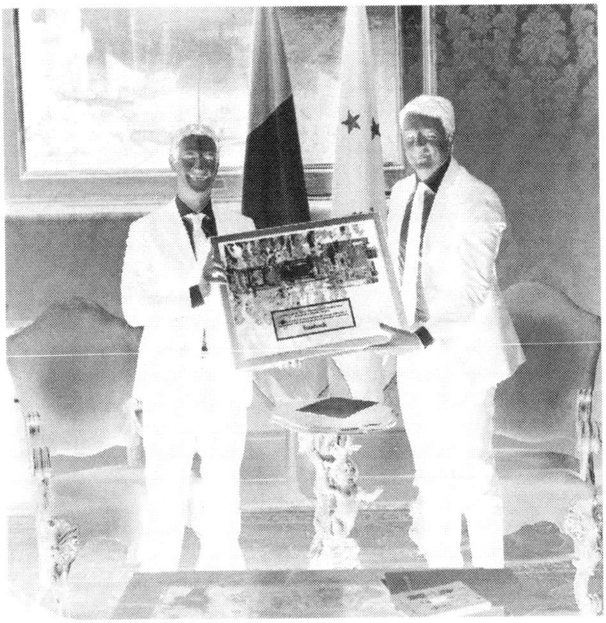

2 PEOPLE, PEOPLE SMILING, PEOPLE
STANDING AND SUIT

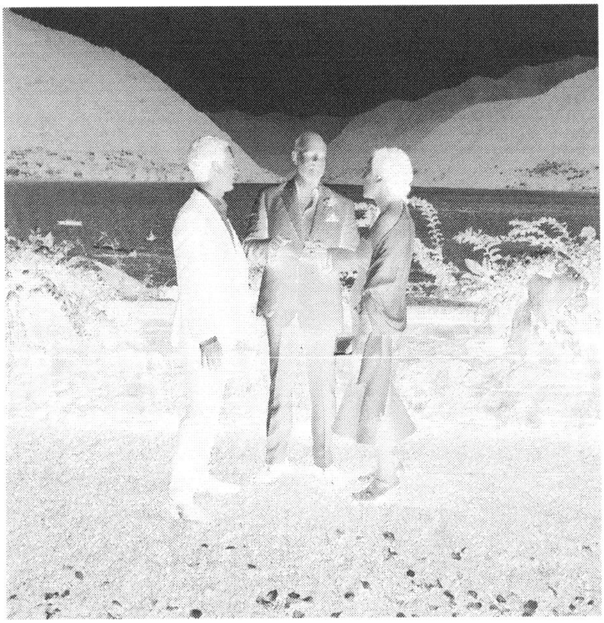

2 PEOPLE, PEOPLE STANDING, OUTDOOR AND NATURE

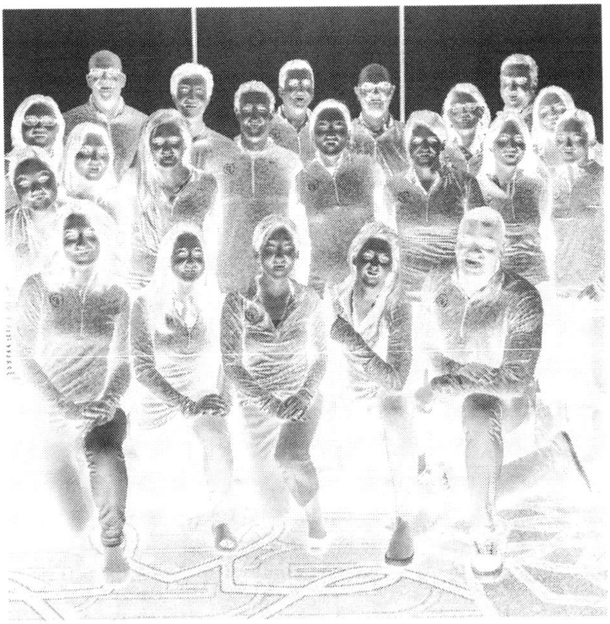

21 PEOPLE, PEOPLE SMILING, INDOOR

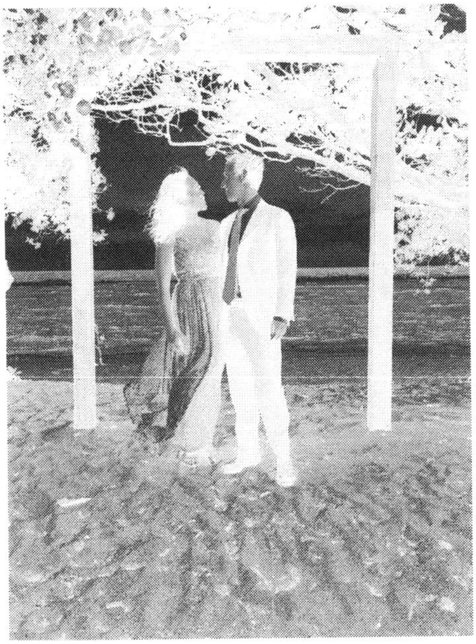

2 PEOPLE, PEOPLE STANDING, OCEAN, SKY, TREE, OUTDOOR AND NATURE

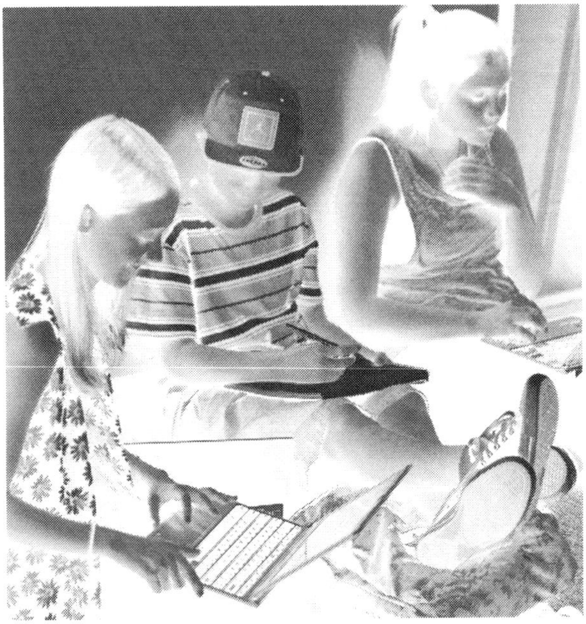

2 PEOPLE, PEOPLE SITTING AND CHILD

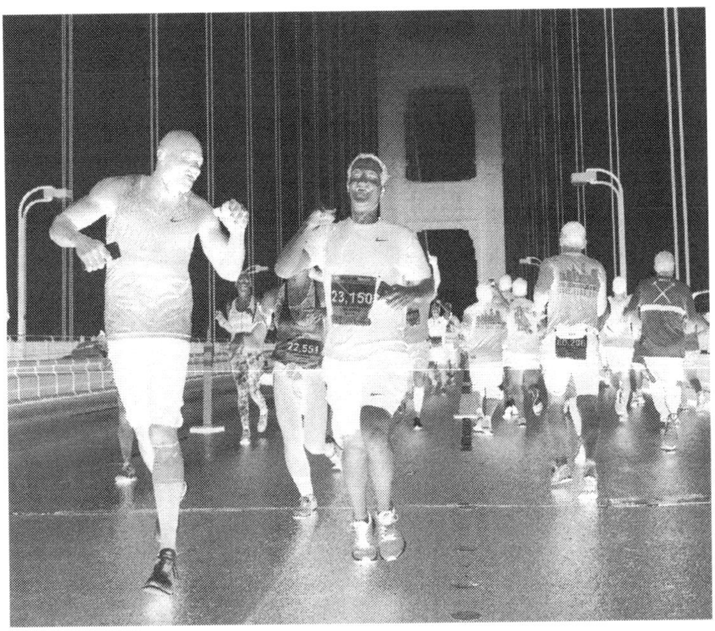
23,150
22,551

2 PEOPLE, PEOPLE SMILING, SHOES,
SHORTS AND OUTDOOR

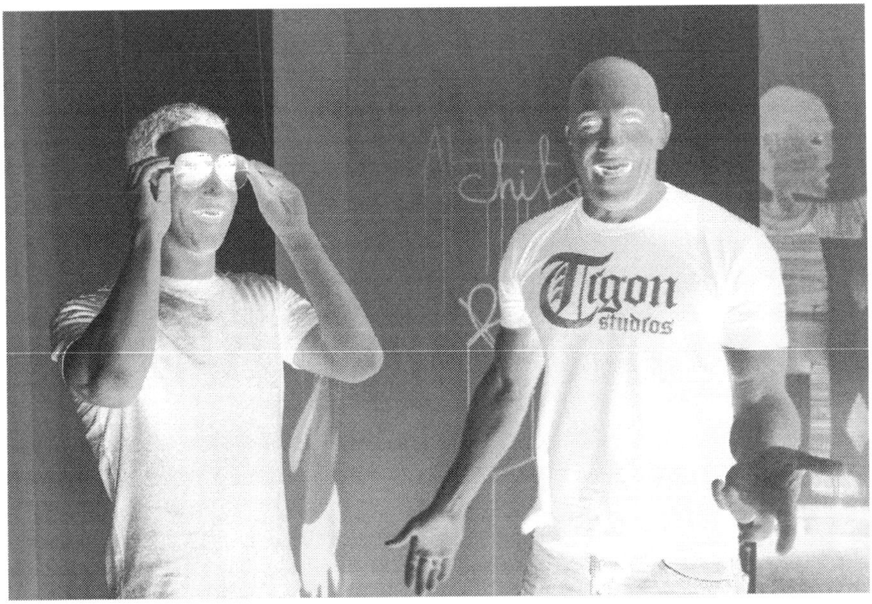
Tigon
studios

2 PEOPLE, PEOPLE SMILING, PEOPLE
STANDING

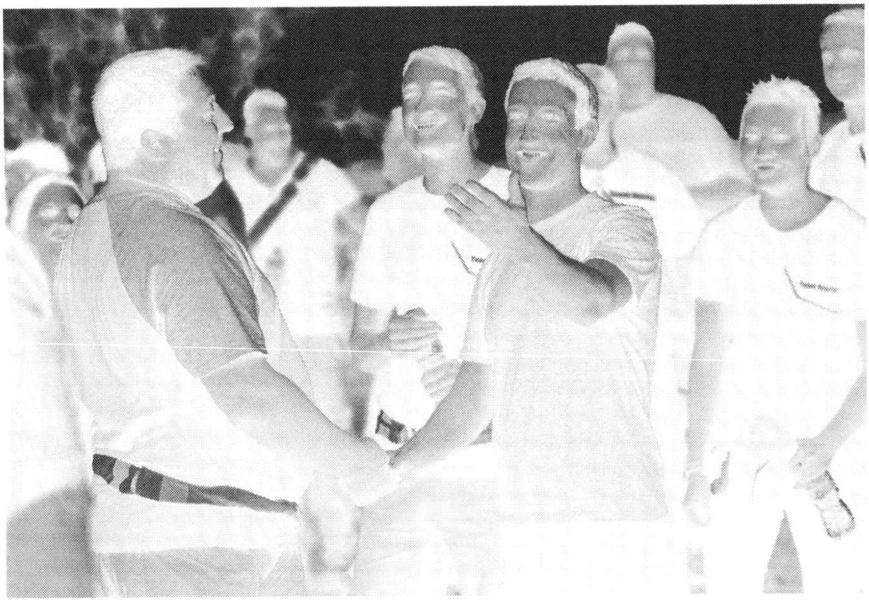

6 PEOPLE, PEOPLE SMILING, PEOPLE STANDING AND OUTDOOR

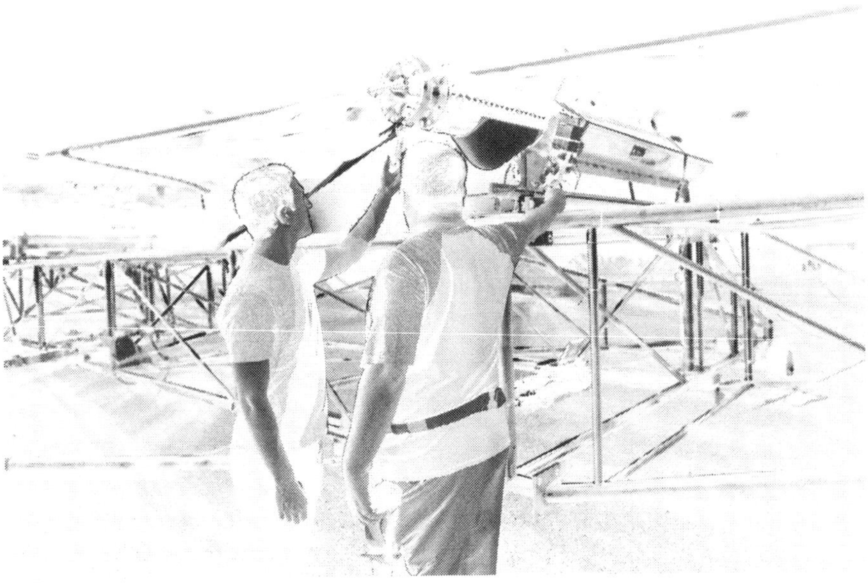

ONE OR MORE PEOPLE AND PEOPLE STANDING

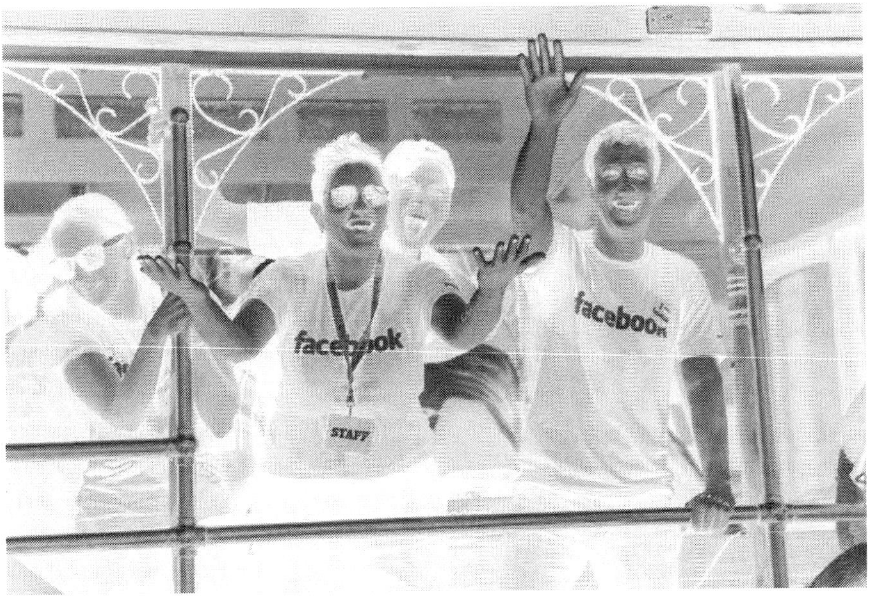
facebook
STAFF
faceboo

4 PEOPLE, PEOPLE SMILING, PEOPLE STANDING

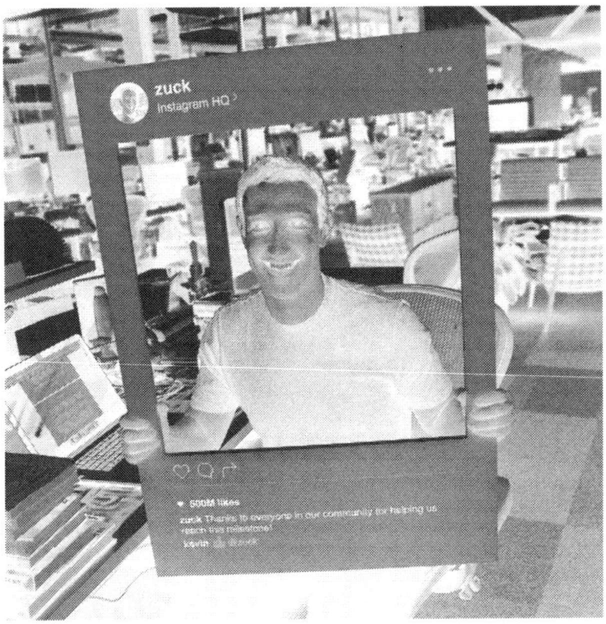
zuck
Instagram HQ

2 PEOPLE, PEOPLE SMILING

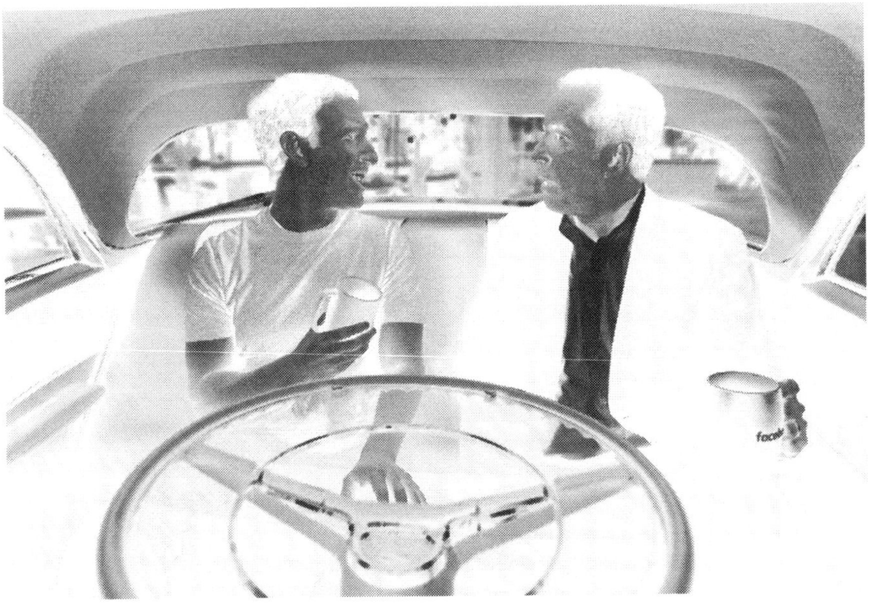

2 PEOPLE, PEOPLE SITTING

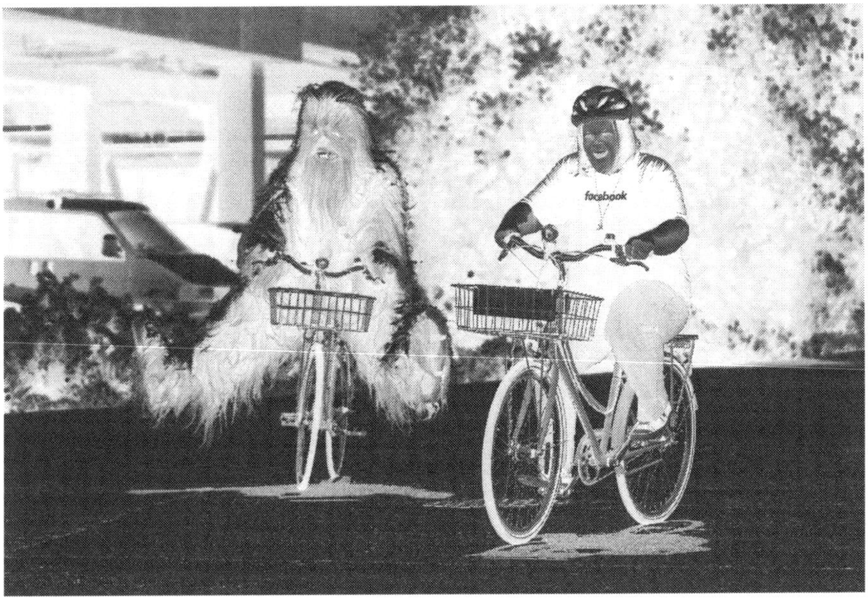
facebook

3 PEOPLE, PEOPLE SMILING, PEOPLE RIDING BICYCLES AND OUTDOOR

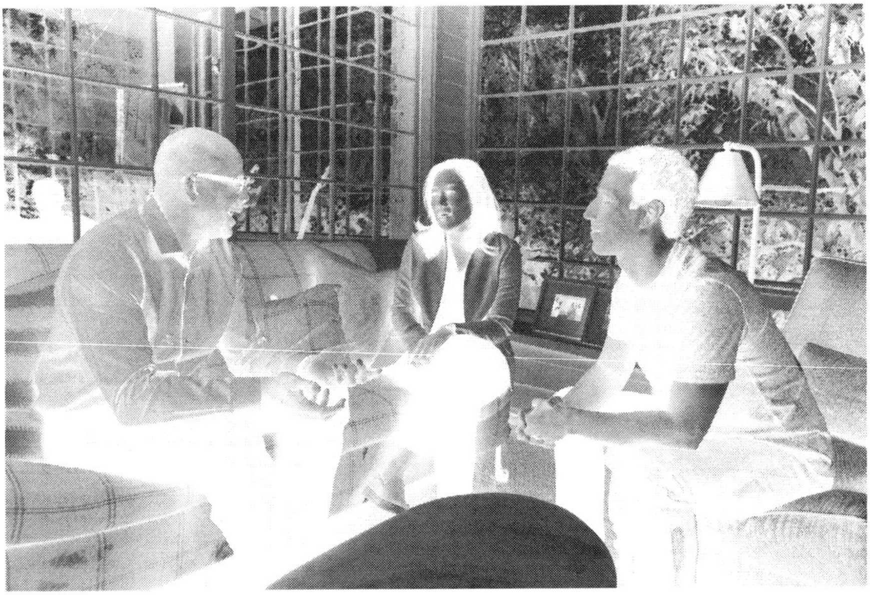

2 PEOPLE, PEOPLE SITTING

APPENDIX:

sample data demonstrating source code location of Automatic Alternative Text and subject matter that challenges the classifier

SOURCE CODE LOCATION

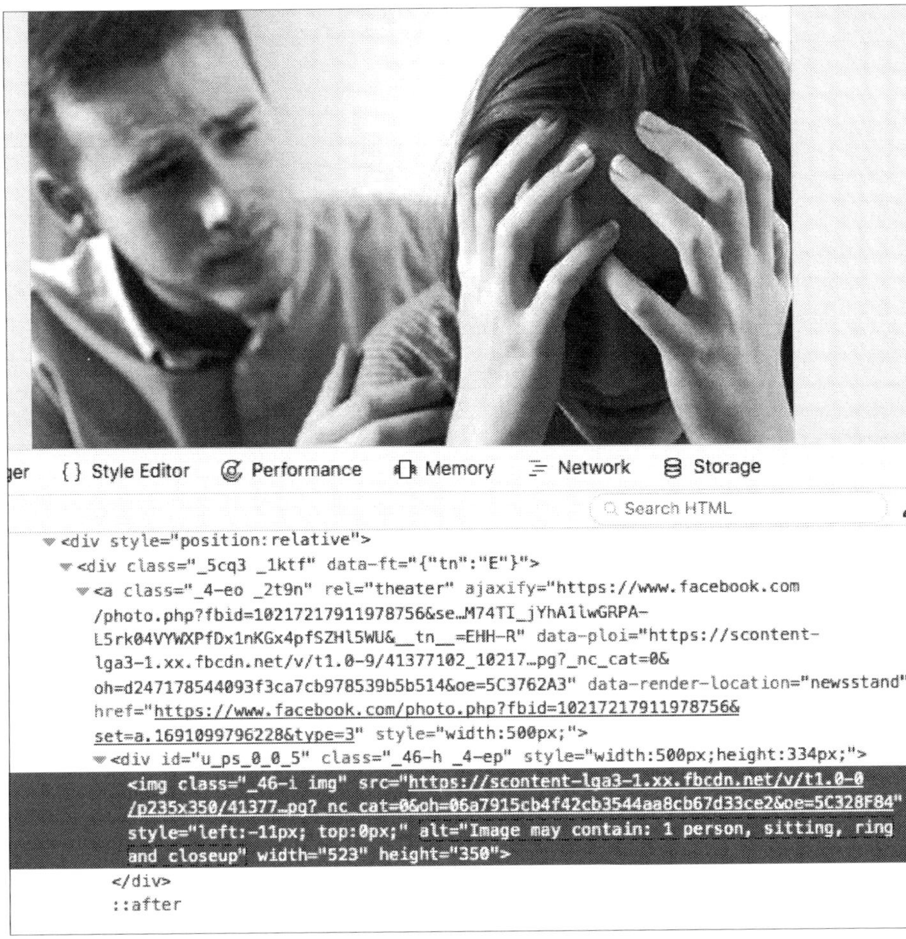

AUTOMATIC ALTERNATIVE TEXT
"IMAGE MAY CONTAIN: 1 PERSON,
SITTING, RING AND CLOSEUP"

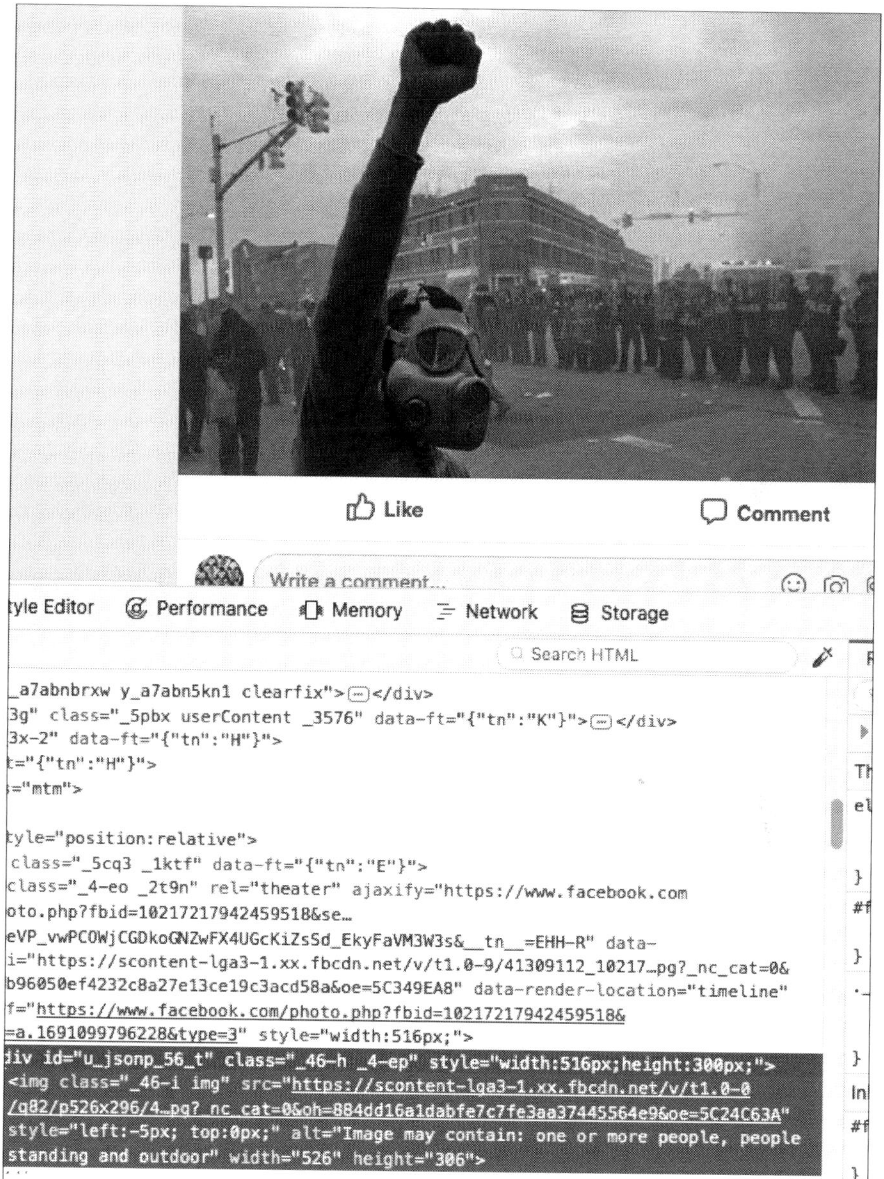

"IMAGE MAY CONTAIN: ONE OR MORE PEOPLE,
PEOPLE STANDING AND OUTDOOR"

The following pages compare image descriptions made by humans and ones generated automatically.

The left column lists captions for stock imagery sampled from the website Shutterstock.com. Because the images were staged with actors and settings that overexaggerate emotions and scenarios, it was assumed they would provide clarity in subject matter for an image classifier. The authors of these images consider search ranking and keywords when describing their work on the site.

The right column lists the Automated Alternative Text that Facebook generated when the same stock images were uploaded to a Facebook Wall. These tests examine the adaptability of the Automate Alternative Text classifier.

seeing like a human	seeing like a computer
PORTRAIT OF AN EXCITED MATURE MAN DRESSED IN SHIRT POINTING FINGER AT BUNCH OF MONEY BANKNOTES ISOLATED OVER WHITE BACKGROUND	1 PERSON, SMILING, STANDING
HAPPY EXCITED SUCCESSFUL BUSINESSWOMAN TRIUMPHING WITH LAPTOP	1 PERSON, SMILING
PORTRAIT OF A HAPPY CHEERFUL WOMAN CELEBRATING SUCCESS WHILE STANDING AND LOOKING AT MOBILE PHONE ISOLATED OVER PINK BACKGROUND	1 PERSON, SMILING
BEAUTIFUL STYLISH YOUNG AFRICAN MALE STUDENT HAVING SURPRISED EXPRESSION AFTER RECIEVING MESSAGE LOOKING WITH BIG OPENED EYES AND MOUTH IN CAMERA BEING HAPPY TO PASS EXAM. SUDDENNESS CONCEPT	1 PERSON, SITTING
FUNNY CHEERFUL BUSINESSMAN JUMPING IN AIR OVER GRAY BACKGROUND	1 PERSON, SMILING
SURPRISED HAPPY BEAUTIFUL WOMAN LOOKING IN EXCITEMENT	1 PERSON, SMILING, STANDING
PORTRAIT OF A CRYING MAN ON BACKGROUND	1 PERSON, INDOOR
DESPERATE MAN	1 PERSON
SAD GIRL CRYING DESPERATELY ALONE SITTING ON A COUCH AT HOME IN A DARK WINTER DAY	1 PERSON, SITTING
YOUNG WOMAN SAD AND CRYING	1 PERSON
TROUBLED YOUNG GIRL COMFORTED BY HER FRIEND. WOMAN SUPPORTING THE GIRL	1 PERSON
A CRYING LITTLE BABY BOY	1 PERSON, SMILING, CHILD, CLOSEUP
DESPERATE WOMAN CRYING	1 PERSON, SMILING

seeing like a human	seeing like a computer
ATTRACTIVE ANGRY COUPLE FIGHTING AND SHOUTING AT EACH OTHER	1 PERSON
ANGRY ASIAN CUTE GIRL SCREAMING AFTER HER MOTHER TAKE A TABLET AWAY. STRESSED CHILD, KID WITH ATTENTION DEFICIT HYPERACTIVITY DISORDER (ADHD) CAN'T HANDLE HER EMOTION	1 PERSON, SMILING
ANGER, CLOSE UP OF ANGRY MAN WITH SMOKE COMING OUT FROM HIS EARS	1 PERSON, BEARD
ENRAGED TROUBLED MAN SCREAMING IN ANGER, CRAZY AND MENTAL	1 PERSON
SCREAMING, HATE, RAGE. CRYING EMOTIONAL ANGRY WOMAN SCREAMING ON BLUE STUDIO BACKGROUND. EMOTIONAL, YOUNG FACE. FEMALE HALF-LENGTH PORTRAIT. HUMAN EMOTIONS, FACIAL EXPRESSION CONCEPT. TRENDY COLORS	1 PERSON
THE ANGER AND SCREAMING MAN	1 PERSON
YOUNG WOMAN VOIMITING IN THE BATHROOM	ONE OR MORE PEOPLE AND PEOPLE SITTING
MAN SUFFERING FROM SICK STOMACH AND VOMITING	ONE OR MORE PEOPLE AND PEOPLE SITTING
YOUNG VOMITING WOMAN NEAR SINK IN BATHROOM	ONE OR MORE PEOPLE
FEAR OF FLIGHT. SHOCKED MATURE BUSINESSMAN TOUCHING HIS HEAD WITH HANDS AND LOOKING AT CAMERA WHILE SITTING AT HIS SEAT IN AIRPLANE	2 PEOPLE, PEOPLE SMILING
YOUNG MAN ISOLATED ON GREY BACKGROUND DRESSED IN CASUAL CLOTHES, COVERING MOUTH WITH HANDS AND ROUND EYES EXPERIENCING DEEP ASTONISHMENT AND FEAR	1 PERSON, CLOSEUP

seeing like a human	seeing like a computer
A SCARED BUSINESSMAN HIDES FROM TWO GIANT SHADOWS OF HUMAN HANDS REACHING TO HIM. FEAR OF UNKNOWN. UNRELIABLE PARTNERSHIP. NEW BUSINESS VENTURE	1 PERSON, DANCING AND SHOES
SCARY WOMAN AFRAID OF SOMETHING IN THE DARK	ONE OR MORE PEOPLE AND CLOSEUP
STRESSED AND DEPRESSED WOMAN	ONE OR MORE PEOPLE
LONELY AND DEPRESSED ADDICT MAN LYING ON THE FLOOR OF HIS HOME FEELING MISERABLE AND ANXIOUS	ONE OR MORE PEOPLE
UNHAPPY LONELY DEPRESSED WOMAN AT HOME, SHE IS SITTING ON THE COUCH AND HIDING HER FACE ON A PILLOW, DEPRESSION CONCEPT	ONE OR MORE PEOPLE
SERIOUS MAN IN BEDROOM	ONE OR MORE PEOPLE
DEPRESSED TEENAGER SITTING HOLDING HEAD IN HANDS, STRESSED SAD YOUNG WOMAN HAVING MENTAL PROBLEMS, FEELING BAD, NEED PSYCHOLOGICAL HELP, ADDICTED HEARTBROKEN GIRL EXPERIENCING ADOLESCENCE CRISIS	ONE OR MORE PEOPLE
DROWN BETWEEN WORKSHEETS	ONE OR MORE PEOPLE
PRECARIOUS	ONE OR MORE PEOPLE
DROWNING MAN IN SEA ASKING FOR HELP WITH RAISED ARMS	ONE OR MORE PEOPLE, SWIMMING, OCEAN, WATER
3D RENDER OF A GREAT WHITE SHARK ATTACKING A FEMALE SWIMMER (WITH DIGITAL PAINTING)	NO AUTOMATIC ALT TEXT AVAILABLE
YOUNG BUSINESSMAN TRAPPED INSIDE UNCOMFORTABLE SMALL BOX	1 PERSON

seeing like a human	seeing like a computer
MAN CAUGHT IN MOUSE TRAP IN RISK BUSINESS CONCEPT	1 PERSON, SHOES
MAN DROWNED AT THE BEACH IN THE WATER	1 PERSON, SWIMMING, OUTDOOR AND WATER
CHILD NEED HELP. LITTLE GIRL CRYING. PORTRAIT YOUNG WOMAN NEED HELP	ONE OR MORE PEOPLE
THE BEAUTIFUL BUSINESS WOMAN AT OFFICE ASKS OF THE HELP	1 PERSON
VICTIM CIRCUMSTANCES.MAN WHY NEED HELP.	1 PERSON
FIRE IN THE HOUSE	1 PERSON
LAPTOP DAMAGE. LAPTOP ON FIRE AND FLAMES. COMPUTER REPAIR. FLAMING FIRE LAPTOP COMPUTER.	FIRE
FIRE SHOW, DANCING WITH FLAME, MALE MASTER FAKIR WITH FIRE WORKS, PERFORMANCE OUTDOORS, FLAME CONTROL MAN, A MAN IN A SUIT LED DANCES WITH FIRE, DRAWS A FIERY FIGURE IN THE DARK	ONE OR MORE PEOPLE, FIRE AND TEXT
STRONG AND BRAVE FIREFIGHTER GOING UP THE STAIRS IN BURNING BUILDING. STAIRS BURN WITH OPEN FLAMES.	FIRE, NIGHT AND TEXT
FIRE IN THE HOUSE	ONE OR MORE PEOPLE, PEOPLE STANDING, FIRE AND TEXT
FAMILY MOTHER WITH CHILDREN AT BURNING HOUSE FIRE ACCIDENT BACKGROUND FIRE IN THE KITCHEN	FIRE AND NIGHT
SHOCKED MAN LOOKING AT BURNT COOKIES WITH SMOKE COMING FROM OVEN	1 PERSON, INDOOR

seeing like a human	seeing like a computer
FIRE FIGHTERS PUTTING OUT A HOUSE FIRE BIG FIRE IN THE BUILDING	FIRE
FOREST FIRE, SEVERAL HECTARES OF PINE TREES BURNED DURING THE DRY SEASON IN JUNE 2013 IN TELE-SAMOSIR LAKE TOBA (DANAU TOBA) NORTH SUMATRA (SUMATERA UTARA) INDONESIA	NIGHT
YOUNG HIGHSCHOOL STUDENT BUYING DRUGS IN FRONT OF MINORS ON SCHOOL GROUNDS AND IN SCHOOL	1 PERSON, STANDING
POLICE TEAM FOUND HEROIN IN CAR TRUNK OF DRUG DEALER	ONE OR MORE PEOPLE
A POLICE OFFICER FINDS DRUGS DURING THE SEARCH OF DRUG DEALERS	ONE OR MORE PEOPLE, PEOPLE SITTING AND SHOES
TWO OLDER DEALERS WEIGHTING MANY KILOS OF DRUGS INTO A PACKAGES	1 PERSON, SITTING AND INDOOR
SNUFF DRUGS AND A RIPPLED MONEY BANKNOTE	ONE OR MORE PEOPLE AND PEOPLE SITTING
YOUNG MAN IS TAKING DRUGS IN A DARK ROOM. HAVE GUN AND MONEYS IN THE WOODEN. CRIME, SOCIAL PROBLEMS, DRUGS, DARK LIFE, SELECTED FOCUS, VINTAGE STYLE	ONE OR MORE PEOPLE, TEXT AND CLOSEUP
TWO DEALERS PACKING IN ROOM LOT OF DRUGS FOR DISTRIBUTION	ONE OR MORE PEOPLE, PEOPLE SITTING, FOOD AND INDOOR
DRUG DEALER IN A TUNNEL. A DARK PLACE TO DEAL PERSON	ONE OR MORE PEOPLE
CLOSE UP OF PERSON COOKING HEROIN USING LIGHTER	ONE OR MORE PEOPLE

seeing like a human	seeing like a computer
BULLETS ON DOLLAR BANKNOTES WITH WHITE DRUG POWDER	ONE OR MORE PEOPLE AND TEXT
DRUGS USER PREPARING DRUGS TO USED WITH RAZOR BLADE	"NO AUTOMATIC ALT TEXT AVAILABLE."
BRUTAL DRUG DEALER TAKES PACKED DRUG	ONE OR MORE PEOPLE
BRICK OUT OF THE SUITCASE AND CUTS IT WITH A KNIFE TO TRY A SAMPLE. HE SQUATS IN THE ABANDONED BUILDING WITH BOARDED UP WINDOWS	ONE OR MORE PEOPLE
BEAUTIFUL WOMAN IS TYPING SOME ANSWERS TO CUSTOMER. CHARMING BEAUTIFUL WOMAN IS DRUG DEALER. ATTRACTIVE GIRL SELLS THE DRUGS ON INTERNET ONLINE AND SHE IS ADDICTED DRUG OR NARCOTIC	ONE OR MORE PEOPLE
Young Man Dealing Drugs From Car	2 PEOPLE, OUTDOOR
TOP VIEW IMAGE OF THE DRUG DEALER WAS ARRESTED IN HANDCUFFS, HAS STACK OF BANKNOTE, GUN AND PACKAGE POWDER OF DRUGS ON WOODEN TABLE, DRUGS CONCEPT IN DARK VINTAGE COLOR STYLE	ONE OR MORE PEOPLE
POLICE ARREST DRUG TRAFFICKER WITH HANDCUFFS. LAW AND POLICE CONCEPT	ONE OR MORE PEOPLE AND SHOES
HAND OF ADDICT MAN WITH MONEY BUYING DOSE OF COCAINE OR HEROINE. DRUG ABUSE AND TRAFFIC CONCEPT	ONE OR MORE PEOPLE